HOW TO SOLVE

BRENDA ROGERS lea͏
in private practice, a teacher at the University of Kent's
School of Continuing Education, and as an art teacher
and artist. She trained with the Marriage Guidance
Council (now 'Relate') as a counsellor and group
facilitator, as a Gestalt therapist with the London
Growth Centre, as a supervisor of counsellors and
therapists with Metanoia and as an artist for one exciting
year at Canterbury College of Art. She also qualified as
a teacher of adults by taking a diploma in adult and
further education when she was 'rather too old' at 54.
All these happened after she had brought up a family of
three children and cared for ageing parents-in-law.

Overcoming Common Problems Series

For a full list of titles please contact
Sheldon Press, Marylebone Road, London NW1 4DU

Beating Job Burnout
DR DONALD SCOTT

Beating the Blues
SUSAN TANNER AND JILLIAN
BALL

Being the Boss
STEPHEN FITZSIMON

Birth Over Thirty
SHEILA KITZINGER

Body Language
How to read others' thoughts by their
gestures
ALLAN PEASE

Bodypower
DR VERNON COLEMAN

Bodysense
DR VERNON COLEMAN

Calm Down
How to cope with frustration and anger
DR PAUL HAUCK

Changing Course
How to take charge of your career
SUE DYSON AND STEPHEN HOARE

Comfort for Depression
JANET HORWOOD

Complete Public Speaker
GYLES BRANDRETH

**Coping Successfully with Your Child's
Asthma**
DR PAUL CARSON

**Coping Successfully with Your Hyperactive
Child**
DR PAUL CARSON

**Coping Successfully with Your Irritable
Bowel**
ROSEMARY NICOL

Coping with Anxiety and Depression
SHIRLEY TRICKETT

Coping with Blushing
DR ROBERT EDELMANN

Coping with Cot Death
SARAH MURPHY

Coping with Depression and Elation
DR PATRICK McKEON

Coping with Stress
DR GEORGIA WITKIN-LANOIL

Coping with Suicide
DR DONALD SCOTT

Coping with Thrush
CAROLINE CLAYTON

Curing Arthritis – The Drug-Free Way
MARGARET HILLS

Curing Arthritis Diet Book
MARGARET HILLS

**Curing Coughs, Colds and Flu – The
Drug-Free Way**
MARGARET HILLS

Curing Illness – The Drug-Free Way
MARGARET HILLS

Depression
DR PAUL HAUCK

Divorce and Separation
ANGELA WILLANS

Don't Blame Me!
How to stop blaming yourself
and other people
TONY GOUGH

The Epilepsy Handbook
SHELAGH McGOVERN

**Everything You Need to Know about
Adoption**
MAGGIE JONES

**Everything You Need to Know about
Contact Lenses**
DR ROBERT YOUNGSON

**Everything You Need to Know about
Osteoporosis**
ROSEMARY NICOL

Overcoming Common Problems Series

Overcoming Common Problems Series

Overcoming Common Problems

HOW TO SOLVE
YOUR PROBLEMS

Brenda Rogers

SHELDON PRESS
LONDON

First published in Great Britain in 1991
Sheldon Press, SPCK, Marylebone Road, London NW1 4DU

British Library Cataloguing in Publication Data
Rogers, Brenda
    How to solve your problems.
    1. Problem solving
    I. Title
    153.43

    ISBN 0–85969–629–4

Photoset by Deltatype Ltd, Ellesmere Port, Cheshire
Printed in Great Britain by Courier International Ltd, Tiptree, Essex

Contents

Introduction

I am a counsellor in private practice and a teacher of adults at my local university and adult education centre. I teach courses on how people learn, on assertiveness, on coping with stress, on creativity and thinking skills and on problem solving. So a great deal of my time is spent in looking at various kinds of problems and finding ways to solve them. As a counsellor I was trained not to solve people's problems for them but to help them to find ways to solve them for themselves, so I've looked for self-help methods to pass on to people for many years.

Many of the theories of psychology, especially what is called Humanistic Psychology, are in themselves good ways of describing and understanding and solving problems. So I've put together those that seem to have worked well for me, for people I've worked with, and for the people who come to the problem solving workshop days we run at the University of Kent's School of Continuing Education.

My thanks are due to Bob Selman who taught me how to experience my feelings, to Edward de Bono who taught me how to use and value the lateral direction of thinking that was natural to me and to Hugh who won't allow me to be illogical or to deceive myself.

Brenda Rogers
September 1990

1

Stepping Back

Self awareness and introspection. Good problems; not all problems are bad. Your strengths as a problem solver. Problems as challenges.

At some time in your life you may have had a problem that seemed to take over: no matter how you tried to forget it, the problem stayed with you, day and night; you became so absorbed in it that you found it hard to think clearly about it; if you talked about it to friends, their ideas and solutions seemed impossible; it was almost as though the problem was a part of you – so much so, that you could hardly see how it could ever be solved or overcome.

Or, you may remember a time when life seemed nothing *but* problems: as fast as you tried to sort one out, another one came along. They began to pile up, thick and fast, so that even when one was solved another one or more took its place. Soon you began to feel that it was hardly worth making any effort: you would never be clear enough of problems to have the time and space to think positively about your life.

Self-awareness and introspection

In this book I hope to be able to give you some ideas that will enable you to stand back from whatever it is that seems insoluble at the present and to take a fresh look at it.

But you may feel that it's impossible to distance yourself from your own life: 'How can that happen?' you may say. 'I can't split myself into two people, me and not-me, and then expect not-me to observe myself.' Fortunately, most people possess this ability in their imaginations. Our minds are wonderfully flexible and we use that self-consciousness often – though more frequently to criticize than to help ourselves. If someone asked you now to think of the things you do well and the things you do badly, I'm sure you would be able to think very quickly of many faults you have, but unless you're an unusually self-confident person it

1

would take you a little longer and much more effort to list all the things you do well! Now think about what you are doing right now, as you read this book. How are you sitting or standing? Are you relaxed or tense? How are you feeling? Are you interested, puzzled, suspicious, cautious, hopeful?

So, try to become a little more self-conscious than usual and look at yourself, your life, your ambitions and your values. Then, try out some of the exercises in the book to see if you can learn to be a more efficient solver of problems. Each chapter will suggest some action for you to take yourself. The first is below:

ACTION: Because problem-solving is a skill that can be developed with practice, start off by thinking of a problem that you solved in the past. Try to remember the stages you went through:

the time you thought it was insoluble;

the ideas you had about solutions;

what made each of the solutions impossible;

how and when you had the brainwave that solved it for you, or the circumstances that changed and sorted things out for you;

how you put your solution into practice;

whether it was easy to sort out or whether you still had to put some hard work in to resolve the situation;

whether you remembered afterwards how difficult it had seemed at the time and whether you had ever praised yourself for solving it. If not, do so now!

Problems as challenges

The sorts of problems that this book might help you with are personal problems, relationship problems, organizational problems and creative problems. Not all problems are bad, so we will look at the possibilities for finding really interesting problems. An artist friend of mine says that all creative people need an axe to grind, a problem to solve. Scientists search for really interesting problems for research. Without problems life would be dull and we would lose our flexibility and our ability to survive. If you can learn to look at even serious problems as challenges and as interesting puzzles to be overcome or absorbed, then you will acquire a positive attitude to your life and be a resourceful friend to other people when they, too, are troubled. This is not to suggest that you become detached or cold in your problem-solving, only that you stand back for a time in order to look at the whole picture. When you have decided what you want to do, then, of course, you step back into your life and bring all your emotional and intellectual and physical energy to bear on the matter. I hope that some of these ideas will help you to use all these aspects of yourself wholeheartedly.

Someone in one of my problem-solving workshops said that the exercises seemed far too many and detailed to solve the small problem that she had brought. It was explained that the exercises were intended to be like the 'Pick-and-Mix' sweet counter in Woolworth's. So, help yourself to anything that seems useful and leave out the parts that aren't for you. They may well be useful at a later date with a different kind of problem.

2

Clearing the Ground

Writing a 'case study'. Questions to ask yourself: Do you really want to solve the problem? Is it really your problem? Are you using one problem to disguise another? Could someone else help or solve it for you?

Writing a 'case study'

You have now decided to step back a little to take a clear objective look at the problem you wish to solve. That can be difficult when you're emotionally involved. Writing a case study is a way in which you can help yourself over that difficulty. Read the example on this and the next page before you start on the action in the next 'Action box'.

ACTION: Take a pen or pencil and a sheet of paper and imagine that you are writing an account of someone else's problem, not your own. Write down what your problem is, who is involved and describe the circumstances. Try to keep your account as simple as possible. Pretend that you are a social worker or counsellor or a helpful official who has to describe the 'case'. You, of course, are the 'client'.

Here is an example:

Rosa has a row with her ex-husband every time he comes to collect their three children to take them out for the day. Tarrant, her ex-husband, is devoted to the children and comes to see them regularly, but he brings his girl-friend, Irene, with him every time. As Tarrant left her for Irene, Rosa finds this intolerable; she just doesn't want Irene in her flat and Rosa's mother says she is foolish to allow her to come. She tells Tarrant he can't take the children out any more unless he comes alone. The children are upset and accuse their mother of spoiling their relationship with their father.

Rosa writes the following 'case study':

Problem:

the client (Rosa) is having difficulties with her ex-husband and doesn't want him to see their children except on her terms.

People involved:

client

client's mother

client's ex-husband

ex-husband's girl-friend

children (3): 2 boys, 1 girl

Circumstances

client dislikes ex-husband's girl-friend and does not want her in the flat or to associate with her children. Client's mother says she has every right to object. Ex-husband will not come without girl-friend and refuses to wait outside for the children. Children ought to see their father and they want to see him.

When you have written your account, put it aside for a time and do something else. Then pick it up again and try to look at it as though this was a situation that was happening to someone else. You may find it helpful to invent new names for the people involved in your problem, and for yourself, so that you can look at it as dispassionately as possible.

In this chapter we are not intending to find solutions, merely trying to discover some of the things that can get in the way when we are faced with a problem. So, with your 'case-study' before you, see if any of the questions below will help you to clear the ground before you set out on the problem-solving trail. If one of the questions leads at once to a solution, you can put this book aside until the next problem appears!

Questions to ask yourself

1. Do you really want to solve the problem?

At first this seems to be a ridiculous question: no one wants problems! But think again. Carl Jung, the psychologist, suggested that there can sometimes be an advantage in *not* solving a problem: it can be easier to put up with a trying situation than to set about the difficult and sometimes emotionally painful work of changing the situation. Or you may be so accustomed to difficulties that you can hardly imagine life without them. Perhaps you feel that you deserve a hard life. Unfortunately, people who have been treated unkindly when they were young tend to believe that they somehow deserve to be treated badly all their lives; if you have never known anything else you expect the worst. If this is your experience it could be that you haven't tried very hard to solve problems and, strange as it may seem, almost dread not having any problems because they are so familiar. Or, you may be gaining some advantage from the problem itself.

To return to Rosa's case. Rosa's mother is very supportive and attentive to Rosa. Rosa often feels lonely bringing up her children on her own. When she rows with Tarrant she knows that her mother will be very protective and sympathetic towards her. She also knows that several of her women friends (particularly those who have suffered from broken relationships or marriages) enjoy talking about how bad men are, and that they too will rally round and be attentive and sympathetic. But there is another advantage in the rows with Tarrant. Rosa was deeply hurt when Tarrant left, and it is easier for her to blame his girl-friend than it is to face the painful fact that their marriage was never very happy. So the rows about the girl-friend get rid of many of Rosa's hurt and angry feelings.

2. Is it really your problem?

Some people need to feel valued and useful. They spend a lot of time sorting things out for other people for a variety of reasons. Rosa's mother is trying to live her life through her daughter. A lonely widow, she finds the drama of Rosa's problems more exciting than her own hum-drum life. She also enjoys feeling needed by Rosa; it reminds her of when Rosa was a child and brought all her problems to her mother. So, unconsciously, she makes things worse by encouraging Rosa to be angry, even though she genuinely believes that she is helping Rosa to solve the problem of Tarrant's visit.

It is good to help other people when they ask you to and want you to. But people also need to feel able to work things out their own way if they are to develop. There are few things in life more satisfying than having solved a really difficult problem. We know this instinctively when we stand back to let children discover for themselves how to cope with difficult situations.

So, make sure that the problem really is yours and if it isn't give it back to the person it belongs to, gently but firmly.

3. Are you using one problem to disguise another?

What Rosa hasn't faced up to is that far from wanting to stop Tarrant taking the children out she sometimes wishes that he would take them away altogether. Although she loves them dearly, they can, like all children, be difficult sometimes. Bringing up three lively children on her own and holding down an interesting but demanding job is exhausting. The responsibility of making all the decisions alone is also hard and it doesn't help when the two older children are often argumentative and defy her. She worries, too, that they really need a father. But all these feelings are very uncomfortable; she is a good mother and if she was asked if she really wanted the children she would be outraged and insist that of course she did. So it's easier to go on being angry with Tarrant than it is to acknowledge that she feels inadequate and bad-tempered with the children sometimes.

4. Are you creating a problem when there needn't be one at all?

Do you need to keep this problem for fear of losing face, or because you won't back down when you know you're in the wrong? Would a little tolerance or common sense solve the problem? You could try asking a good friend if you think this applies to you.

Rosa could put up with Tarrant and his girl-friend. It would be slightly unpleasant for her, but it's only five minutes or so once a fortnight, and it would give her a peaceful day to herself once in a while. So all Rosa stands to lose is the mixed pleasure of saying unpleasant things to Tarrant and Irene and the support of her mother and friends when she recounts the latest scene in the battle.

5. Can someone else help you to solve the problem or solve it for you?

There's nothing wrong with asking someone for help and a person who isn't involved with the situation can sometimes see a solution when you can't. There are many agencies who can help with problems; the Citizen's Advice Bureau is a good place to start since it's free and they have information on all the agencies and organizations that have been set up to deal with a wide variety of problems. So, if it's a problem about a relationship that isn't working out, or a practical problem to do with your job or your home, complaints about services or goods, legal matters, finding a new doctor or dentist or an organization to help people suffering from a specific disability or illness, or a whole host of other things, the CAB will usually know someone or some place where you can get advice. If you haven't a friend or a colleague or a relation to talk to, is it possible to seek the co-operation of any of the people who are involved with the problem itself?

The last people Rosa thought of asking for help were Tarrant and Irene. But after talking the problem over with the personnel officer at the firm she worked for, she asked Tarrant, Irene and her mother to come round one evening to discuss the matter properly. It wasn't easy at first, but the two older children joined in and Rosa began to see that Irene was genuinely fond of the children and they were fond of her. She felt rather jealous of this new friendship but decided that it was better for the children not to be at the centre of all the rows. Her mother went on being difficult but Rosa gradually took a firmer line with her mother and got her to see that the children's welfare was the most important issue.

ACTION: Some hard questions to ask yourself.

Look back at your 'case history' and decide whether the person whose problem you are studying (yourself, of course, but go on pretending it's someone else's story) has answered these questions honestly:

1. Does the person really want to solve the problem?
2. What advantages are there in keeping the problem?
3. Whose problem is it? (List all the people responsible for the problem and decide who is responsible for what)
4. Is there another, deeper problem that matters more than this one?
5. Is this problem being used to distract from the deeper problem?
6. Does this need to be a problem at all?
7. What would be lost if the problem was solved?
8. Who could solve the problem or help to solve it?

3

Defining and Clarifying
the Problem

**Objectives and obstacles. Wants and needs. 'Won't' or
'Can't'? Breaking the problem down into smaller, manageable problems.**

Objectives and obstacles

A simple way of looking at a problem is to say that it is a
combination of 'objectives' and 'obstacles'. The 'objectives' are
what you want to happen and the 'obstacles' are whatever is
stopping that from happening. So it can be helpful to look at the
problem with those two things in mind. Sorting out objectives
and obstacles helps you to be clear about what exactly the
problem is. Getting the problem definite and clear is sometimes
the key to finding a solution, since it's very easy to become
confused about the issues surrounding a problem.

Let's take a look at a problem situation and see how that might
apply:

Danny and Marilyn live together in a terraced house, which
means that they have a very narrow garden at the back. They
both go out to work so they haven't much time for gardening.
To make life easier they paved the back garden and planted a
border of flowering shrubs at the back. The shrubs have done
well and look very beautiful in the summer. The only problem
is that in the six years they have lived there their neighbours'
large tree has grown very large and now a low-growing branch
hangs right across their garden, so they can't see their shrubs
in the summer. They asked the neighbours to cut the tree
down but they refused.

Danny and Marilyn's objectives: to see their shrubs from the
house and to be able to sit in their garden in sunshine, not
shaded by the tree.
Obstacles: the tree; the neighbours' refusal to cut it down.

ACTION: Make a note of what your objectives are in the problem you're wanting to solve and what obstacles are in the way of you getting them.

Let's look at the objectives more carefully. Marilyn loves to sunbathe so she feels that it's perfectly reasonable to want to sit in her own garden in the sun. But presumably the neighbours like their tree so *they* want to sit in its shade. Who matters most? If we divide the objectives into 'wants' and 'needs' we might be able to clarify matters.

Wants and needs

What is the difference between a 'want' and a 'need'? You could say that you *want* a swimming pool in your garden, but it's probable that you don't *need* one. If you had a medical condition that could only be cured by swimming every day, then you might feel justified in saying that you *needed* a swimming pool. Similarly, children *need* a balanced diet to keep them healthy, but they might *want* to live on chocolate bars! These might seem terribly obvious, but if you listen to other people talking you'll soon discover that wants and needs are often confused. It might be useful for you to think for a moment of all the things you *need*, like food and shelter and affection, and then of all the things you *want*, some of which you might get and some of which you know you will never have.

ACTION: When you feel clear about the difference, list the things you want and the things you need in relation to the problem you are working on.

In a problem situation we find very often that two sets of people want different things to happen but it's hard to decide who has the most right to get what they want. But if one of the sides really *needs* something, that would usually be more important than mere *wants*. Of course, here, we are talking about what is right and fair and moral; there are totally selfish, unfair and immoral people who are determined to have their own way whatever the cost to someone else, but in that case we could at least be clear about who was in the right!

In Danny and Marilyn's case, they *needed* one particularly large, low-growing branch of the tree removing because it was rubbing against the fence and seemed likely to break the fence down if it wasn't removed. It hung down so low that they couldn't put garden chairs out without it brushing their heads. They thought that perhaps there was a legal right to remove branches that hung over their garden, but they couldn't see that their neighbours *needed* to have the tree growing into their garden at all. Although they *wanted* the tree removed altogether, they realized that that might be too much to reasonably expect. They were also interested in the environment and were beginning to think that perhaps the tree was needed by the birds and insects, and by the people in the neighbourhood, since it was the only large tree around.

Having looked at objectives and needs and wants, let's look again at the 'obstacles':

Danny had not been particularly tactful in his complaint to the neighbours, nor had he been particularly clear about what he wanted. In fact he hadn't said what he wanted at all. He'd seen the elderly couple in their garden and had shouted 'What are you going to do about this tree? It's ruining my garden, it's an absolute eyesore, I'm sick of all the leaves!' The neighbours had looked anxious and said that they liked the tree very much, that they had planted it fifty years ago and that no one else had ever complained, and then they went indoors. So it wasn't certain that they wouldn't agree to its being pruned, but it seemed obvious that they didn't want to cut it down.

Are you clear that other people involved in your problem really know what you want? Have you taken their needs into account?

'Won't' or 'can't'?

We've seen that Danny and Marilyn hadn't been clear about

what exactly they wanted (what their objectives were) and hadn't made their objectives clear to their neighbours. Because the neighbours hadn't offered to do anything about the problem, Danny and Marilyn had assumed that they wouldn't want to. It was almost as though the elderly couple had said 'No, we won't'. But maybe the real reason that they had not offered to discuss it was because they felt that they couldn't do anything about it. They were pensioners so maybe they couldn't afford to pay someone to prune the tree and weren't strong or agile enough to do it themselves. We can often assume that someone is saying that they *won't* do something when the truth is that they *can't*; they are not able to, not capable enough or don't know how. Some people are too proud to admit this so they'll say 'No' and pretend that they don't want to do whatever has been asked of them.

In the example above, the neighbours had been frightened, so they had just avoided the whole issue. And, by assuming that the neighbours wouldn't discuss it, Danny and Marilyn had also been confusing 'won't' with 'can't'. When they said: 'We can't get anywhere with the people next door!' they would have been more accurate to say: 'We won't talk to the people next door about this'.

In fact, with any problem, it's a useful exercise to try substituting the word 'won't' for 'can't'. Even if the changed word isn't accurate it can give you a clue about what your real feelings are:

'I can't tell this person how I feel'. 'I won't tell this person how I feel'.
'I can't bear to cope with this'. 'I won't cope with this'.
'I can't let this happen'. 'I won't let this happen'.

Sometimes the 'won't' is a more honest expression of your feelings. Similarly, when you feel that you are determined not to give way, try changing 'can't' for 'won't':

'I won't think about it'. 'I can't think about it'.
'I won't give in'. 'I can't give in'.

ACTION: Make a list of objectives with needs separated from wants, and a list of obstacles which includes other people's needs and wants, and makes clear the difference between can't and won't. Then make a list of things you lack information about.

What Marilyn and Danny need is information – on how to prune trees without killing them, on whether the neighbours actually agree to the tree being cut down or pruned; what the legal rights are about overhanging branches and about shading someone else's garden; and where the tree or branches could be disposed of if agreement were reached. We'll be looking at ways to get hold of information in the next chapter.

Breaking the problem down

Now we can break the problem down into more manageable portions and that may help us to become a lot clearer about what the real problem is. These are the ones Marilyn and Danny need to tackle:

1. Communicate with the neighbours. This would be useful in other future situations as well as now.
2. If the neighbours agree, find out who could prune/cut down the tree (gardening firm; offer to do it themselves; where to get tools; who else would help; where to dispose of branches).
3. If they don't agree, find out legal rights (Citizen's Advice Bureau, solicitor, neighbourhood law centre, Town Hall). Also find out if there is a preservation order on the tree.
4. If decide to cut overhanging branches off, how to cope with resentment from the neighbours (Can someone talk to them? Can we put up with it?).

Of course, if Marilyn and Danny felt that they couldn't cope with being unpopular with the neighbours, then this might be the biggest obstacle to their achieving their objectives.

Here is a check list for you to define and clarify your own problem and break it down into more manageable portions. You

13

may not need to respond to all the sections, and you may need to add some of your own.

Objectives:
- What do I want to happen (my ideal solution)?
- What do I need to happen (the very least I can settle for)?

Obstacles
- What do other people want in this situation?
- What do other people really need in this situation?
- What I won't do is . . .
- What I can't do is . . .
- What they won't do is . . .
- What they can't do is . . .

Breakdown of the problem:
- To solve this problem I will need
    - to be clear what the problem is
    - practical information or advice (see also Chapter 4)
    - help/support (who from?) (see also Chapter 5)
    - equipment
    - more ideas (see Chapters 6 & 7)
    - to talk to other people involved when I am clear what the problem is/listen to other people involved to understand their views.

ACTION: Make a list of all the things you will need to do to sort out the problem and then do *one at a time*. If you're anxious, it's much better to do things gradually and it's very satisfying to solve things one at a time. Just getting hold of practical information can give you a sense of achievement that will carry you on to the next stage of the process. Give yourself a pat on the back for every step you take.

Marilyn and Danny's first step was to find out what the legal position was. They discovered that they had a legal right to cut off any overhanging branches and that they were required to return the branches to the tree's owner. This made them feel much surer of their ground and less angry with their neighbours. They invited their neighbours in for a cup of tea and showed them how the branches of the tree shaded their kitchen and overhung their garden. The neighbours were surprised as they'd never seen the tree from the other side of the fence. They agreed that it needed pruning but explained that they couldn't afford to do it themselves. Danny organized a group of friends to help him prune off the overhanging branches and the local school were glad to have the wood for a bonfire night party they were organizing. Marilyn and Danny had a much better relationship with their neighbours after this; although they never became friends they were able to discuss problems about shared fences without either side getting angry or upset.

4

Collecting Information

The four functions: thinking, feeling, sensing, intuition. Starting points for practical information.

In the case we looked at in the last chapter it became obvious that one of the difficulties in problem solving can be lack of information. And it's not just the information that we *know* that we lack, it's the information that we just didn't know existed or that we had never thought of asking for. How often has it happened that after a problem situation is over someone says: 'If only I'd known . . . I could have solved that problem for you.' You see on television just the tool that would have stripped off the wallpaper, or hear on the radio of the organization that could have helped you with transport for a disabled friend. So is there any way we can get to know the things we don't know at the time when we need to know?

There is another aspect to the information problem, and that is having enough information about ourselves. You may be one of the fortunate people who understand themselves well, so you will have plenty of information about you. But many people are frequently surprised at their own reactions. Have you ever thought 'It's not like me to feel like that'? Recently a very old friend of mine died. I took the news very calmly. I thought: 'Yes, he's gone, I won't see him again' as though that was the most ordinary thing in the world. The next day I remarked to a friend that I seemed to have lost my ability to have feelings; being someone who knew me well she said she thought that unlikely and had I suffered some shock? It was three or four days before I became deeply sad and I'm still not sure whether I was sad underneath all the time or whether it took those days for the sadness to begin. The theory is that we feel things subconsciously but block them from conscious awareness. I know that theory well, and it is likely that I *was* sad underneath, yet I was unable to feel any sadness. I tell this story because I spend a lot of time thinking about my feelings and doing the kinds of exercises I suggest later in this book. I would assume that I know as much

16

about myself as anyone, and yet still have to take the trouble to be certain about what I'm really feeling or about what I really want and need.

Personal awareness

Jung's four functions

There is a fairly simple way to make sure that you are bringing the whole of your personality to bear on a problem. Jung, who I mentioned before, thought that the human personality could be seen as the operation of 'four functions'. The four functions are: thinking, feeling, sensing and intuition. As we go through these I suggest you examine your present problem with each of these functions to discover if there are any that you have missed or avoided. Jung thought that we tend to develop one or two parts of our personality more than the others, so if you find that you don't use one of these aspects very often you will almost certainly discover that you are extra good at one of the others.

Thinking This is probably the most obvious part of problem solving: we think about the problem. But when Jung talked about thinking, he was talking about the intellect and the intelligence, the logical and rational parts of our minds. We can say: 'I've thought about this problem for weeks' when really we mean that we have *felt* about this problem for weeks. The last chapter was largely about thinking, about knowing the difference between certain ideas that we have. If you worked through the 'Actions' parts of the last chapter you will have been thinking about your problem in some fairly organized ways.

Feeling This is to do with the emotions, not to do with the sense of touch. Feelings are very important in problem solving. Even some very intelligent people are not good at people-problems because they forget to take feelings into account. Managers used to be trained in giving orders and putting the good of the company and its profits before the good of individuals. Nowadays there is a movement towards training managers to manage people; to understand their feelings and to try to make their jobs interesting and rewarding. We still have a long way to go in really caring about people in organizations, but at least it

17

has been recognized that if people are unhappy they will not work well or swell company profits! So, taking note of your own and other people's feelings can be the key to solving some problems.

Check whether you have considered the emotions of any other people involved in your problem. Then think about your own feelings: Can you give them a name? The emotions we most commonly feel are *anger*, *fear*, *sadness* and *grief*, and *happiness*, from quiet contentment to joy. What feelings do you have in relation to this problem? If you're not regularly in touch with your emotions, this could be hard to answer, so give yourself time. Equally, if you tend to live through your feelings rather than thinking things out carefully, you may get one feeling mixed up with another. The commonest mix-ups are feeling as if you're angry when really you are afraid or sad, and feeling as if you're afraid, fed up or tearful when underneath you're really angry. In twentieth century Britain it is generally men who feel that they are not allowed to cry, be gentle or show fear and women who are taught that anger is ugly and unfeminine, so they cry rather than be assertive or aggressive.

Sensing This is the function with which we are aware of what are generally called the 'five senses', though I think there are more than five. The five senses people generally list are: seeing, hearing, smell, taste and touch. The extra ones that don't quite form part of these are: the sense of temperature, which tells you the warmth or coolness of yourself and your surroundings (some people think this is a part of the sense of touch); the sense of gravity and knowing whether we are right way or upside down, allied to which is the sense of balance; and the kinaesthetic sense, which is all the bodily sensations of moving joints, muscles or tendons, which tells us what we are doing physically.

A lot of Western people are out of touch with their senses. If you spend your life in a city, in crowded buses and streets, you learn to live in your own thoughts and don't react to every person that passes you by; life would be impossible if you did! In the film *Crocodile Dundee* the hero tried to speak to all the people he passed in the street in New York. The fact that it seemed so funny shows how we have to learn to ignore people and events and noise and bumping into people if we are to survive without becoming totally exhausted. Our senses can only take in so much information at a time so we learn to concentrate on the things that are important (like traffic lights and not getting run over), and ignore a great deal of what is happening around us. This very useful gift we all have of shutting out unnecessary things has the less welcome effect of making us sometimes unaware of things that are important.

So how can you be sure you've brought your senses into problem solving? Well, practical information comes through our hearing or seeing, so check if you've actually *read* any documents or operating instructions. Did you *listen* to what someone else was saying or were you preoccupied with your own thoughts? Did you *notice* the other person's expression when they were speaking? We give a lot of clues to our inner thoughts in the way we stand or sit. Shrugs, nods, frowns, secret smiles, glances can all show attitudes that the person might not otherwise want us to know about. Allan Pease's book *Body Language* (Sheldon Press) can tell you a lot more about these unconscious gestures, but you'll need to learn to watch and see them before you can understand them.

It is possible when thinking back over a situation to find that you have seen and heard more than you had realized at the time. Think back over any situation concerned with your problem and make a note of how people were looking, what exactly they said and the tone of voice they said it in. The actual words used in a dispute, for example, can be very important. Was there anything in the room that was important? What clothes were people wearing? How did you feel in your body? Were you tense and uptight or did you make large gestures? Did you move around or did you feel glued to the spot?

Intuition This is the sense that many people distrust or even don't believe exists. And yet some people practically live their whole lives on intuition alone. I find the idea of intuition even more useful if I include the whole of imagination, fantasy, dreams and creativity when I'm trying to sense what I intuitively feel about a person or situation. I think most people at one time or another have had a hunch about something and it turned out to be right in the end. When people are thinking of moving home, they very quickly feel that a particular flat or house is OK or not-OK for them. Even more strongly, the way we choose our partners seems to be far more by intuition than by any practical considerations. People who interview others for jobs say that when they choose someone because they feel instinctively (our word for intuitively) that s/he'll fit in to the organization, that person is very rarely unsuitable. If someone is chosen who has all the right qualifications but who is felt to be not quite right for the job they often tend not to be. I have heard many personnel officers and managers say this, and I've certainly experienced it myself on the few occasions I've interviewed people. So if you don't usually go by your hunches, try to guess what you might feel about your problem if you weren't an intelligent, aware, feeling person! You might find that there are some unfair or prejudiced ideas lurking in the back of your mind. Just for once, allow yourself to think them. Don't feel that you must act on them, but allow the thoughts/feelings/ideas/whatever they are, to surface so that you can consider them as part of the information you are collecting.

I mentioned imagination and fantasy. Both can be very useful when assessing a situation. Let your mind day-dream about the problem: think of fantastic solutions; imagine how it would be if the problem were solved – How you would feel? What you would do? It can be particularly valuable when trying to get in touch with your intuition to harness your senses as well and imagine how your body would feel if the problem was solved. Would you feel more relaxed or more alert and alive? Imagine going for a walk with the problem no longer on your mind. How would you walk? If you met someone you knew, how would your voice sound, what might you say?

Dreams are another source of help. They tend to connect with whatever is on our minds. So write down any dreams you have and see if they can give you any new slants on your problem. You may discover that you are angry or feel caught or confused or inadequate. The kinds of feelings associated with a dream can give us clues to intuitive feelings that we wouldn't ordinarily realize that we had.

I also mentioned creativity as a part of intuition. We'll look at that in more detail in Chapter 7. Creativity is a difficult thing to write about because, like intuition, it isn't a part of us that works from our conscious, thinking minds, and of course I have to write

20

to the conscious thinking part of you since this is a book and you are reading words on a page, which is a thinking kind of activity. To use your creativity as part of the information gathering process, you might try doodling. Write a word that seems to be an important factor in your problem. Then start to turn it into a pattern. Don't think about what you are doing; listen to the radio or talk to someone or think about something else. When you've spent some time doing it, put it away for a time, at least overnight. Then look at it the next day and see if it suggests anything to you.

ACTION:

- *Thinking* Have you thought about your problem as logically and reasonably as possible?

    Look back over Chapter 3 and check if you've worked out objectives and obstacles and wants and needs.

- *Feeling* What emotions does this problem bring for you?

    What sort of emotions are affecting other people involved?

- *Sensing* What are the facts?

    What do you see when you look at other people involved?

    Do you listen or only hear what they say?

    What tone of voice do you use when you speak to others involved?

    How do you feel in your body (tense, relaxed, mixed-up?) when you try to deal with the problem?

    How would you feel in your body if the problem were solved?

- *Intuition* What hunches do you have about the situation?

    If you had to guess the outcome of this situation, what might it be? What fantastic solution could you invent?

    What sort of dreams do you have when the problem is on your mind?

Having looked at these four aspects of your self, make yourself a life map. You may have become a lot clearer about your objectives in this problem, but probably have never considered what your objectives in life are. You may find that a friend would be interested in doing one as well; you can then talk them over together. It usually takes between half and one hour.

ACTION: The idea is to think of your life as a journey and that you are now going to make a map of your journey. Take a fairly large sheet of paper or the back of a cereal packet, and a pen or pencil. It's fun to use coloured crayons if you have some. Start off with your birth and draw a picture of something that occurs to you about it. You don't need to be artistic, some people just use blobs of colour to suggest a mood, or matchstick people, or a symbol like a heart or a teardrop. You can put words in or leave them out, whichever appeals to you. Now draw in the path or road your life took. You can have it going up and down for ups and downs in life, whatever you feel will depict the way it went. Try to put in all the important things that happened to you, good and bad. Don't worry if you can't remember all of it, most people have some vague patches. When you get to the present, continue, into the future. You can have fun imagining how your future life could be, since it doesn't have to be realistic. Some people depress themselves by saying: 'I know it's going to be awful' but that isn't the idea of the map at all. The idea is to map out for yourself a really interesting future so you can discover what you would really like to happen. The hardest part for some people is going right on until they put in their own death as well. But why not? It's the one thing you can be sure of. You can plan a really peaceful end for yourself, or a dramatic one if you prefer that. If death is too heavy for you, end it with old age and some clouds of not knowing after that. One group became really interested in where they would like to be buried and what they would like to have written on their gravestones.

When you've completed the map, put it away for a day or two, before getting it out again. See if you notice any patterns in it. We'll be looking at patterns later, but for the present, just check whether your ideal hopes for the future are impossible to achieve. Even if they aren't, are there any aspects of your ideal future that could be achieved?

Now try writing down some slightly more realistic hopes for the future. Then look again at the objectives in your current problem. If you're trying to sort things out in ways that would help you to achieve your long-term objectives, well and fine. But if you are trying to achieve things that don't match up with your long-term aims, maybe you need to spend some time thinking about how you want to spend your life and what you really want and need. Having long-term aims in life and knowing what they are is a very important piece of information that you may not have considered before.

You have taken yourself through the steps of looking at your own self as a source of information about the problem *before* looking at practical sources of information. This you have been asked to do deliberately because many people don't think of themselves as information! Everything you know about the world is in you; if it seems muddled at times then you need to realize that you are operating with muddled information. You will also now have a bit more of your personality available to you; if you were already equally aware of all the four functions then you are a most unusually well-balanced and well-organized person and probably a lot better at solving problems than you care to admit.

So now to look for the more expected sources of information.

Starting points for practical external sources of information

Most branches of the Citizen's Advice Bureau are staffed by volunteers whose aim is to help people to find out whatever they need to know. It is free and it is confidential, so you can ask for an interview and explain whatever it is you want to know and they will do their best to point you in the direction where the information is to be found.

A second very valuable source of information, also free, is your local library. Almost all libraries have an information desk nowadays; if they haven't ask the assistant at the counter. They will have information on an enormous range of topics. Don't forget the encyclopedias and dictionaries, either, or the year-books and all the reference books. If you're not sure how to look something up, ask someone to help you. Never be afraid to ask for help; the worst that can happen is that the person will say 'No' and you may then have to ask someone else.

Another very valuable source of information and help is your local Member of Parliament. Not many people realize that most MPs have a 'surgery' once a week. Find out his or her name from your library and phone for an appointment. Don't worry if you don't share the same politics or if you didn't vote for him/her, s/he is there as your representative and to sort out local affairs. S/he may send you on to your county councillor or district councillor if it is a purely local matter. A hard-working MP has a lot of influence in local affairs and can sometimes achieve things that no one else can do. S/he can be particularly helpful in matters to do with benefits and pensions and also very good at finding out where some help or advice can be sought.

Perhaps the hardest part of finding information is keeping at it! You go to the Citizen's Advice Bureau and they suggest you try the local Social Services. You ring Social Services and explain what you want and they say that they don't do such-and-such, and why don't you try the Red Cross. The Red Cross are only open at inconvenient times and when you finally get there they tell you that they weren't the right people at all and you should try the hospital . . . and so it may go on! When we wanted to hire a wheelchair for a single day it took seven phone calls before we finally found someone who could lend us the folding type to go in a car boot. It would have been easy to give up and say that it was impossible. But this is a book about making things possible and how to get things to happen, so keep at it! Some problems need a lot of determination to solve, and the determination not to be beaten is what solves them!

5

Coping with Obstacles

Looking back. Leaving a problem to solve itself. Getting someone else to solve it for you. Unpleasant alternatives. Accepting the inevitable. Rational-emotive therapy.

The last chapter ended on a very positive note suggesting that you stick with it and become very determined to try hard to solve the problem. This chapter will assume that you're adopting this approach and that you have obtained as much information as possible and therefore some self-understanding.

Looking back: positive or unproductive?

At this point the problem may start to look even more complicated than you had first imagined. If you feel unable to see your way out of the mire you may start to look back to see how this happened in the first place. And it may be that some of the problem was your own fault.

However, it is very important not to blame yourself too much or to feel unduly guilty or helpless. Even if it is true that you got yourself into the situation in the first place, you can't go back in time and change it. You can perhaps only decide never to do such a thing again, and that would be useful for you in the future.

So you made a mistake! We all make mistakes: some small, some enormous. People marry the wrong person; take jobs that don't suit them, join organizations they dislike; agree to do things they don't want to do; offer to do things and then make a mess of them . . . Mistakes are a part of being human; that is how we learn: by trial and error. If you feel that you really need to be angry with yourself, write yourself a letter telling yourself what a terrible person you are, and then put it away and go back to your problem solving. The way to show yourself that you're genuinely sorry is to do something positive, and to start to plan ways in which you can put the situation right, even if that means admitting you've been wrong, apologizing to someone, or changing your mind and saying that you've made a mistake. If you're a proud person that will be very hard but it will save you a great deal of time that would otherwise have been spent trying to stifle your regrets or your annoyance with yourself. It will also help to remind you not to behave in a similar way in the future. If you make similar mistakes frequently you may need to talk to a counsellor about this; recurring patterns of behaviour are often a sign that we learned some inflexible ways of behaving as children and need to think about why this happens and whether we can change.

Do what you need to do, then put regrets behind you. You could even try forgiving yourself and remind yourself that you aren't perfect. Look forward to the time when you have sorted your current dilemma out. It is probably true to say that all problems are solved in the long run, even though the people involved are not always pleased by the solution. Decisions *do* get made, think back to the last really difficult problem you had: you *did* decide which job to take; where to go on holiday, or whether to go away at all.

Not *solving the problem as a possible solution*

Sometimes circumstances decide things for us: the person who has been upsetting you moves away from the district, just when you had finally decided to have it out with him!; the second-hand car you were dithering about buying has been sold when you finally make up your mind to have it. Some problems can be solved by the simple but difficult decision of not doing anything about them. And some problems can be solved by asking someone else to cope with them.

There is a commonly held belief that we should face up to our problems. Perhaps for some things that is very good advice. If you've been avoiding noticing that you and your partner seem to be talking less and less and that there seems to be a new coolness between you, it might be very important to face up to the fact that something has gone wrong, otherwise it could just get worse until the relationship deteriorates so much that one or other of you finds someone else to share your joys and sorrows. But most people have also experienced a situation where facing up to things may have made the situation worse:

Maureen and Camilla had worked in the same department store for more than five years. They had met when on a staff-training scheme and although they never met outside work hours they had become good friends, having lunch together two or three times a week and confiding many of their personal problems to one another. Like most people who work in the same organization they gossiped about the rest of the staff, mostly good-humouredly but occasionally maliciously when the gossip was about someone neither of them liked.

Camilla was very upset when the chef in the store's restaurant, Frederic, told her that Maureen was spreading rumours that Camilla was having an affair with her departmental head. Camilla had confided to Maureen that she found her boss very attractive and how difficult it had been for her when he had told her that he and his wife had separated. He often called her into his office to ask her advice and now he wanted to meet her after work. Although she had felt sorry for him she had refused; she was married with a teenage daughter and didn't want to get involved. Her boss was very upset and she was afraid that his need for sympathy plus her own attraction to him might prove too much of a temptation.

Camilla's first thought about the rumours was to fall out with Maureen. She would avoid her, refuse to have lunch with her and hope that this would shock Maureen into seeing how badly she was behaving. But as time went on she became angrier at the thought of how her trust had been betrayed. She thought she would have it out with Maureen. She planned what she would say: 'How could you? I thought I could trust you! You know perfectly well that I had no intention of getting involved with my boss and you knew that I even felt guilty for *not* meeting him when he was so unhappy.'

Fortunately for Camilla she was so torn between silent dignified reproach and furious confrontation that she spent several days trying to decide which was best. She avoided Maureen but found convincing excuses.

Her boss called her into his office before she had made up her mind: 'I hear there is gossip about you and me. I must apologize, it's my fault for asking you in here to tell you about my troubles so often. I had no idea I was compromising you until your friend Maureen came to see me yesterday and told me what was going on. I've decided to go and see a Marriage Counsellor so I won't be loading my troubles onto you in future; I thought I ought to tell you in case you wondered why I won't be asking your advice or asking you to come into my office on your own again. Thank you for being so sympathetic, I'm very grateful.'

Not doing anything saved Camilla from falling out with Maureen who, it seemed, had been a very good friend indeed. She realized that she had been in danger of spoiling a good friendship. She resolved never in future to act on someone else's information but always to make sure that she knew the truth before she confronted anyone. *Not* acting had proved the best solution.

The other problem was the gossip. She wondered whether to ignore it in the hope that it would eventually die down; that would be one solution, and one that would work in the long run. But it occurred to her that the problem was not only hers, and that it could cause far more harm to her boss, Don, than it would to her, since he was still hoping to patch things up in his marriage.

She asked Maureen to come with her to see her boss and the three of them discussed it together. It was quickly obvious that the main purveyor of the gossip was the chef himself. Don thought his motive might be jealousy. Camilla said at once that she would go to see him and explain that she didn't particularly like him and that nothing would persuade her to take an interest in him even if he hadn't offended her and caused her so much embarrassment. The other two decided that it was not a good idea for Camilla to speak to him alone. If he was really jealous he might imagine that this was the way to get her attention.

Maureen offered to go and talk to Frederic; since he had blamed her for the gossip she felt that she also was entitled to an apology or an explanation. There was no way he could deny it to her, since he had told everyone that Maureen had started the gossip. When Maureen tackled him she discovered that their guess that he was jealous was quite wrong; he believed deeply that infidelity was a terrible sin and he had been shocked and outraged by what he saw as immoral behaviour.

But he had behaved very badly in blaming Maureen for the gossip and was very embarrassed when she insisted that he visit every department and explain that his story had been untrue. Once more Camilla was relieved that she had not acted on impulse and confronted Frederic. Maureen was a very calm and capable person and had been able to cope with the situation without making it worse.

ACTION: 1. Ask yourself whether there is a possibility that your problem could resolve itself without your taking any action or making any decision. If you are not a patient person, this could be hard, but it could also be a better way to deal with it; some situations are better not forced. Is it *really* necessary to solve the problem at once? Is it the waiting and not knowing, or the waiting for someone else's decision, that is the real problem getting you down? If you know in your heart of hearts that the problem will resolve itself without your intervention, find something else to distract yourself with until it is sorted out. Use the energy of your frustration to decorate a room or cut the grass or take some exercise.

2. Is there someone else involved, or a helpful friend, colleague or neighbour, who could deal with this situation better than you? If you are a person who likes to resolve their own problems or needs to feel in control of things, this could be hard for you. So put your pride aside and consider if someone else has more information, or knowledge, or skill in dealing with this particular problem. Is there someone who will be calmer or more logical than you could be in this situation?

Unpleasant alternatives

Sometimes the answer to a problem is not what we want:

Paul and Anna have been trying to sell their house for months as Paul has a new and better paid job in another town. Paul has been forced to rent a room during the week and travel home at weekends, which means that he sees very little of his family. The cost of the room and travelling is eating into his savings at an alarming rate.

At long last someone decides to buy the house. Both Paul and Anna are overjoyed until their nextdoor neighbour, a lifelong friend, tells them that the person buying is someone she cannot stand and begs them not to sell to him.

Both of the alternative solutions are unpleasant: losing the sale and making the family suffer both financially and from being apart, or losing the friendship of a neighbour and feeling guilty about leaving her with a difficult situation. The only way to decide is to look at which is the lesser of the two evils. The new owner may not be as bad as the neighbour thinks; he may move again; the neighbour may move herself; the neighbour may be being unfair and have caused the problem herself. If Paul and Anna don't sell, another buyer might arrive tomorrow. This would be the only possible good outcome for them, but the chances of that happening are very slight. So, regretfully, they decide that they simply cannot afford to lose the sale. They tell their neighbour and hope that being a good friend she understands the dilemma. If not, then they will have to accept that they have lost a friend, but gained peace of mind and happiness for themselves and their family.

One's own peace of mind is important. *Never* write your own needs out of the equation. If you are unhappy you make others around you unhappy too, so your own needs should always be taken into account.

Accepting the inevitable

Some problems cannot be solved. They can be accepted and understood and some people are even able to be positive about such a problem and see it as a challenge. Or they can be the source of frustration and misery. There are incurable illnesses. The problem of disablement is one that can't be 'solved' in the sense of being cured. Of course, people can be wonderfully courageous, they can develop ways to overcome some of the surrounding problems, they can even make an asset of a disability and develop skills that otherwise they wouldn't have bothered with. The long illness of a loved one is not a solvable problem even though some aspects of the illness can be solved. So maybe it isn't a 'problem' at all, maybe it is just a fact of life. There is an old saw which I find useful:

> For every problem under the sun
> There is a remedy, or there's none.
> If there is, try and find it.
> If there isn't, never mind it.

Well, maybe the 'never mind it' is a bit too much to expect. But at least you can give up trying to solve it. So you concentrate on solving all the practical things like support, advice, help, proper diet, equipment, therapy, medication, or whatever else is appropriate to make the situation as easy as is humanly possible for everyone concerned. Doing practical things can be quite helpful if you have an insoluble situation to cope with. But for the main intractable event you need to give up. Give up trying to understand *why* this has happened. 'Why me?' isn't a useful question, 'Why *not* me?' is more so. But maybe there isn't a reason. Consider that you may not have done anything wrong to deserve this situation, or that your blameless life has not been unfairly rewarded with troubles; it is just bad luck and very unfortunate. Shakespeare has Hamlet say, very wisely, 'There is no armour against adversity.' There is no way we can prepare ourselves for misfortune. No one can predict where lightning will strike, who will be ill, which roof will be blown off in a gale, whose parents will become helpless and whose will live to a healthy old age, whose child will be born disabled, which country will be stricken with drought.

Becoming adult means learning that you are not invulnerable. Anything can happen to me: one day, I will be old; one day I will die; those I love will not live forever. There may be difficult times to come, so enjoy the good times when they are here: appreciate good friends, loving relations, kindly colleagues, they will not be there for ever. And when things go wrong, accept events with as good grace as you can muster. It's not just a moral issue, it's for your own healthy survival to accept those things that cannot be changed. Otherwise your mind is fighting your inclination constantly, your energy is drained away, and you become bitter and lose the very friends you need for support. The situation is here, it is with you, it cannot be changed. Accept it and commit yourself to doing your best with it. Denying that it exists just doesn't work; when you least expect it it will come back to you, stronger than ever.

Rational-emotive therapy and 'musturbation'

Albert Ellis, inventor of rational-emotive therapy (RET), suggests that people have an unconscious list of what they feel *must* be so. He calls them 'musturbations'. One of them is that people feel that things absolutely must be fair, reasonable and logical and that if they are not it is absolutely horrible, dreadful and awful and that they cannot and will not cope with them. But, as he points out, there is no rational reason why this *must* be so. Life is often unfair, unreasonable and illogical, and if we look at our experience of life we will see that this is often so. Yet we go on believing that things *ought* to be different, that there *ought* to be someone or something that will make these fair, reasonable and logical things happen. It seems likely that we pick up these ideas in childhood and tuck them away in our minds and never look at them again to find out if they are true in our experience. These irrational beliefs, beliefs that are not borne out by experience, can be the root source of our inability to accept difficult facts and situations.

ACTION: Do you feel that somehow, almost magically, your difficult situation should be solved for you, or should never have existed in the first place, or that someone, somewhere, should have noticed you and selected you as the person who should *not* have to endure this difficulty? There is *no* such magical solution. You were not chosen to have this situation, neither as reward for good- nor punishment for bad behaviour. The situation has happened and is here as much as the sun is in the sky and the leaves grow on the trees. It is a part of being human, to have problems and difficulties; you are human so you are a part of these events.

6

Creative Thinking

Generating ideas. Brainstorming. Dreams.

Brainstorming

This is another constructive part of problem solving: looking for new ways of tackling a problem.

Take a large sheet of paper, write your problem at the top, then put down *every single idea* that comes into your head when you try to think of a solution. That means including all the sensible, practical, logical ideas that you have, plus all the irrational, silly, nonsensical and impractical ones. If you do this with a friend or in a group, make sure that you don't discuss any of the ideas or argue about them or even consider where they might lead to; just write them down regardless. Apart from helping you to open your mind this can be very useful for expressing feelings; it can also lead to a lot of laughter if you try to think of sillier and sillier solutions. At this stage in problem solving being lighthearted is very valuable as it can free you from the kind of emotional blocks that may have stopped you from finding a solution before.

Let's look at a very ordinary problem:

Janette is a very tidy person. She likes to keep all her papers in order so she has a cardboard box in which she keeps the electricity bills, the gas bills, water bills, rates and community charge bills. She also keeps the receipts for the clothes she buys and for anything else that might go wrong and need to be taken back to the shop she bought it from. She's planning to start her own business soon so she wants to get her private papers organized before she begins. After a year the box gets very full and the papers aren't so easy to find as they're all mixed up together. So how can Janette sort out the papers?

How can I sort out my papers?
Let's start with sensible answers. You can probably think of more than I am listing here!

Buy a concertina file.

Put each month's bills in a large envelope and mark it with the month.

Put all electricity bills in one envelope, all gas in another and so on, then keep envelopes in alphabetical order.

Get some small boxes to put each type of bill in.

Clip all the same kinds of bill together.

Number each bill as it arrives, keep in numerical order and make file cards to identify which bill is which.

The last one seems a lot of work, so lets look at some silly solutions next:

Employ someone else to do it.

Stop using electricity etc. so I won't have any bills.

Go and live in a country where the state pays for electricity etc.

Colour gas bills green, electricity bills emerald, clothes bills cobalt blue, rates red, etc.

Sort through the lot every time I need one.

Spread them out all over the floor so I can see them all.

Stick them all over the walls with bluetack so they'll come off again when I need one.

Employ a magician to find the one I need by magic.

Give them all to an accountant to deal with everything for me.

Marry an accountant or a filing clerk.

Force someone else to be my slave and sort them for me.

Memorize every one and where it is in the pile.

You'll notice that some of these ideas are suggested by the one before; once you get into the swing of it you'll find that your imagination can make up some really ridiculous solutions.

The next step is called 'paradoxical intention'. In this we try to think of ways that Janette could make the problem worse!

Throw them all out of the window.

Chop them up and mix up the bits.

Crumple them up into balls so you can't see what each one is.

Put them face down on the floor.

Don't even keep them in the box, mix them up with other papers.

Shut your eyes and pick one out at random.

Buy lots of things so you have even more bills.
Collect other people's bills as well.

Now try 'seeding'. Take a word that has nothing at all to do with the problem and see what ideas are suggested to you. Take the word 'breakfast', for example:

Keep the papers in cornflakes packets.
Stick similar bills together with marmalade.
Sort the papers first thing in the morning.

Now we go back to the original problem and look at each word in it – '*How can I sort out my papers?*' – very critically.

'*How?*' By what method? Is there a method Janette doesn't know about? Is there someone who knows *how* to organize papers? Is there a book on it? Is 'how?' the real question? What about 'why?' Why should she bother? Is it important? Does it really matter?

Change 'how?' to 'when?'. When can she sort out her papers? Maybe it won't be necessary until there are a lot more of them. Or maybe she should have started a system a long time ago. Perhaps she should put them into a system as they arrive rather than wait and sort them later.

Change 'why' to 'where?' Where could she sort them out? Looking back at the 'How to make it worse?', perhaps on the floor would be better than trying to get them into piles on a small table.

'Which?' is another word we could try. Which papers should she sort out? That would lead us to the idea that the paid ones might not need much sorting, especially the ones that had been paid some time ago.

'*Can*' Can she or can't she? Maybe she isn't capable of doing it and needs some expert help.

'*I*' brings us back to ideas about who could do it best, maybe not 'I' but someone else. Or the thought that 'we' would be better, so maybe Janette could ask a friend or pay someone to help her to do part of the job even if not all of it.

'*Sort*' This is the crux of the problem. What sort of bill? What sort of paper? How to tell the difference between them?

Which matters most, the date they were paid or the service or goods they were paid for?

'*Out*' is interesting. Maybe some of them could be taken out of the box; perhaps the older ones could be thrown away. Should there be separate boxes for unpaid bills and for recent bills?

'*My*' Is it her responsibility, are all the bills hers? In this case, we will suppose they are, though we can see that the problem would be different if they weren't. And if someone else has a similar problem with their papers, maybe they could be asked for advice.

'*Papers*' Do they have to be paper? Could she copy the older ones on a computer. Could she pay by credit card and then only keep the credit card statements? Could she get them all copied on microfilm so they wouldn't take up much room? Could she make a list of all the other bills she paid by cheque and the date she paid them then throw the bills away and rely on bank statements and her list if there was any problem?

One idea sparks off another even as the 'brainstorm' is being completed. So the endstage is to look at all the ideas put down and to see if there are any ideas that could connect or lead to possible solutions. Some of Janette's ideas were: Old bills wouldn't be so likely to be needed again, so the old bills could be thrown out; the colouring idea suggested she could mark recent bills in felt-tip pen in the colour she chose for that category as they arrived and then keep them in a box or envelope coloured the same colour. Since she was thinking of starting her own business, the idea of spending even more money made sense. It would probably be sensible to buy a filing cabinet to help her keep proper accounts and keep bills in order. The idea of scrumpling bills up and throwing them around for some reason made her think of cornflakes spilling from the packet, and until she could afford a filing cabinet she decided to keep each category of bills in cornflakes packets with the tops trimmed off and painted in the correct colour.

ACTION: Do your own brainstorm on one of the following ideas to get into the frame of mind of thinking up nonsensical as well as realistic ideas. Once you've got the hang of it you can have a go at a real problem of your own. I'm suggesting you try one of these first as it can feel very insensitive and even immoral to be lighthearted about something that is really serious. So bear in mind that these are only IDEAS and that you have no intention of carrying most of them out, you are just freeing up your creativity:

how to get a dog to keep still whilst you bath it;
how to do housework without getting bored;
how to stop a friend from gossiping about you;
what to do on a wet Sunday;
how to cope with too much work.

Dreams

You can use dreams to help you solve your problem. First, make sure you have a note-pad and pen beside your bed, especially if you're one of these people who doesn't remember dreams or thinks that s/he doesn't dream at all. Before you go to sleep, decide that you are going to dream something that will help you to understand and solve your problem. Then as soon as you wake in the morning, write down as much as you can remember of what you dreamed. If you're not in the habit of remembering dreams it might be two or three days before you recall a dream. It doesn't need to be a whole dream, remember, just a fragment of a dream will do.

Jot down what feelings you had: were you afraid, anxious, happy, sad, angry, resentful etc. Often dreams have emotions that don't quite fit in with what was happening, so think carefully about this. Next, write down where the dream took place: indoors or outdoors, in what kind of building or situation. Try to remember if there were any colours in the surroundings and what they were. Now think back to one event and write down exactly what happened, who said what and what you felt, said and did at the time. Write it as though it was a story or a film that you'd seen. Sometimes a lot more details come back to you when you do this. Now, write down any events of the previous day or few days that seem to connect with the dream. There may be no connections with your real life at all, or there might be quite a lot. Finally, write down anything else that the dream reminds you of:

places you've been to, people you know, events that have happened or that you've worried about in case they happened. At this point you may have already decided what the dream means to you; some dreams are very clear and indicate at once that you're more anxious than you knew, that someone is more important to you than you had realized, and many other messages. If there's no immediate message from the dream, or even if there is, put your notes away for a time and return to them when you have time to do this exercise.

ACTION: Imagine that the dream has an identity of its own and that you ask the dream: 'What do you mean, dream?' Write down what the dream says to you. You have to write this as though you yourself *are* the dream.

If the message from the dream doesn't give you any information, you can now start to play a small drama with yourself in which you become each of the characters in the dream. So first you become the setting: the house or room or garden or field where the dream took place. Write down 'I am a garden' if the dream took place in a garden then describe yourself. Now become any other person or object in the dream and write a short account of yourself: 'I am a tree', 'I am a thin man', 'I am a crowd of people', whatever else appeared in the dream. If there is an argument in the dream, write down what each person said. Go on writing down what each object or person in the dream might say and again put your paper away and do something else.

Now you are ready to learn from your dream. Look at each statement and decide if it is really a statement about yourself and your situation.

7

Generating More Ideas

Mind maps. Blocks to problem solving.

Mind maps

ACTION: If you still haven't been able to think of any original solutions to your problem, a mind map or spidergram might be helpful.

To make a mind map, take a sheet of paper – a large one if it's a very complicated problem! Write down your problem in the middle of the paper and draw a line round it. Then start to list all the reasons for the problem occurring in a circle round it. Put in all the causes you can think of, all the people involved, all the events that have added to the problem, each of them enclosed by a line, and each connected to the problem in the middle of the sheet. Then add in all the possible solutions you can think of and connect these to any of the causes or people involved or situations connected with it.

Let's take Diana's problem on whether she should speak up at a staff meeting about something she thought was wrong in the school where she was a teacher:

One of the secretaries had been rather indiscreet and told Diana that there was to be a survey of staffing levels, but that only heads of departments were to be consulted. As a part-time teacher Diana would not be affected, but she felt that the other full-time teaching and administrative staff should be told that the visit of the Divisional Head teacher of the education department the following week was not, as they had been told, a purely routine visit; he was really coming to decide who was competent and efficient and who could be recommended for early retirement or redundancy. Diana

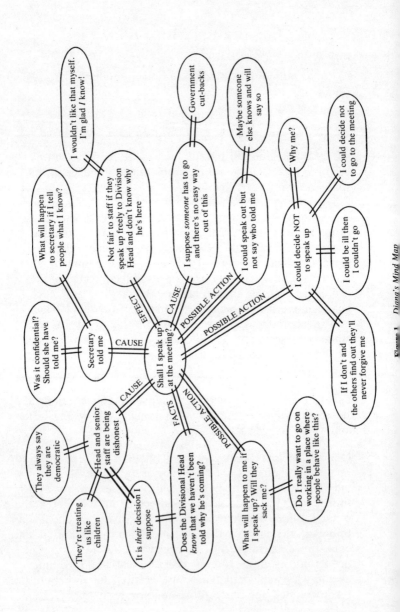

Figure 1 *Diana's Mind Map*

40

didn't want to cause trouble for the secretary, but she also felt that it would be disloyal not to tell her colleagues what was happening. She was angry that the administration and senior staff didn't intend to include them in discussions and were planning to deceive them.

Figure 1 is Diana's mind-map. As she added extra circles, she began to see that although she had thought at first that she was being high-minded in wanting to defend the junior staff, she was really more concerned that other people had a good opinion of herself. Although it was rather painful to admit it, she was worried that other teachers would find out that she had known and failed to warn them. But she was also afraid that the head teacher would see her as a trouble maker and not renew her contract. Part-time teachers only had termly contracts, so it was easier to get rid of them than to get rid of full-time staff.

The mind map seems to work very well for some people in spreading all the ideas out and in making connections between them. It can be useful to put it away for a time and then to add to it later, as more ideas come to you, or to ask someone else to look at it and see if they think you have covered all the possibilities.

Diana looked at her mind map again and saw, almost at once, that there were solutions other than the 'either/or' of speaking up or not. She could go back to the secretary and ask if the information was confidential. She could ring the Divisional Head teacher and ask him if he realized that staff hadn't been told the purpose of his visit. She could speak to one of the senior staff or to the Head and ask them to tell people themselves. Can you think of any other solutions?

What Diana did was to talk with the secretary and tell her that she intended making a formal complaint to the head teacher, *not* saying where the information had come from. She then spoke to the head teacher who was very angry and told her that she had no right to discuss the matter with anyone. This made Diana also angry on behalf of the other teachers. At last she felt clear; since she had risked her own career by speaking out she was certain that her motivation was not purely selfish and now had no doubts that the matter must be made common knowledge. She rang the Divisional Head teacher, who was shocked and surprised that the staff had not been told. He came to the staff meeting himself and the whole matter was discussed openly but very painfully. The head teacher explained that in her view it was kinder for the matter of redundancies to be discussed in private. There followed a most uncomfortable time for Diana and for the whole staff, some of whom supported the head teacher and others of whom lost all faith in her. But the underlying discontent that had made the school a difficult place to work in was at last brought to the surface. Diana felt that she had made the right decision and acted in good faith, even though the outcome was not as she would have liked it to be. But there were no further secrets; the staff were consulted frequently and openly and the school became a much better place to work in. Diana became well respected by her colleagues, some of whom had not been very friendly to part-time staff in the past. She was very surprised to be offered a full-time appointment quite soon after the incident, and although she never after got on well with the head teacher, they managed to establish a reasonable working relationship.

ACTION: Make your own mind map of the circumstances causing and connected with your problem. If this doesn't solve the problem it may at least make some more choices obvious to you. A second stage could be to add to your mind map all the positive things connected with the problem; this may suggest some alternative ways of looking at it.

Blocks to problem solving

When a problem has troubled you for a long time, it's not unusual to feel as though your mind is stuck. You may even have a vague feeling that the answer is there somewhere but you just can't seem to get to it. It's a feeling of being blocked, as though there was a wall between you and the solution.

For example:

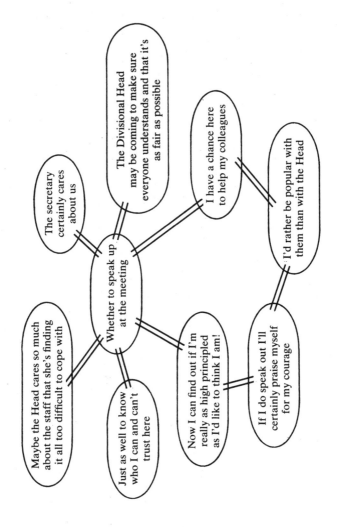

Figure 2. *Positive aspects of Diana's problem*

43

Frank had a loveless childhood and found it very difficult to become committed to a friendship or relationship, but was unsure as to why he felt this way. As a child, dependent on adults, it was a sensible though painful decision for him not to expect love or affection since the lack of it would have been a constant disappointment. The people who should have provided love, didn't, and that was a fact that he had to learn painfully and to accept. Frank not only stopped expecting love, but also forgot that such an emotion was possible. He also had a very deep need for love and was puzzled at his inability to accept affection when it was offered. Wanting and not wanting affection at the same time made him feel very confused and unsure about what kind of person he really was: warm and feeling or cold and rejecting? By discovering what was blocking his emotions and his understanding, he became able to understand himself better and to make decisions that were appropriate for an adult who was no longer so desperately dependent on others as the small child who had been so deeply hurt.

Getting in touch with some of your blocks can be invaluable. There are several ways of doing this; one is to draw a picture of the block:

Sonia is having an exhibition of her paintings later this year and can't seem to motivate herself to finish the two paintings she's started, let alone begin new ones. She started drawing up and down scribbles and then took some of them right to the top of the picture because she didn't feel they were as big as her block; it was as though she had to make them too big to see over. Sonia was surprised that she didn't want to cover the whole paper with them. She left a small gap at the left and a large gap at the right, but that didn't feel quite right until she put in some rather neater vertical lines at each side. She wasn't thinking much about what she was doing [and that's a very good state of mind to be in when you do this exercise] as she had half an eye on a television play that was on at the time, so she was a bit surprised that she had tidied up the smaller lines at the sides until they looked like a fence. Sonia looked at the picture properly and thought that the middle bit looked like a hurdle, the kind horses jump over, and the scrubby bit at the top reminded her of the tops of the huge fences the horses jump in the Grand National. She wondered vaguely if there was water on the other side like Beecher's Brook. Although she did the picture with a blue ballpoint pen, she felt sure it should really be in brown with the round scribbles in green like a plant or creeper growing up the hurdle-fence.

The following day Sonia looked at this scribbly drawing again. She was surprised that her first feeling was that she was quite pleased that the block was made of natural materials: wood and twigs and green-stuff growing. It didn't feel as daunting as it might have had it been made of something hard like brick. The hurdle looked quite flimsy though; she felt she could knock it down quite easily if she really wanted to. The fence made her think that perhaps it was keeping something *out* rather than keeping her in. She had a sense that the hurdle was to stop people seeing in and was a way of keeping her garden private, away from prying eyes. Perhaps if the picture went on longer there would be a gate in the fence, so she could go out and come back in when she wanted to. And she could grow delicate plants against the hurdle; it would be a good shelter against strong winds.

Sonia left the drawing for several hours. During that time it occurred to her that maybe she had had enough of displaying her most private inner self to the world. The pictures she did some years ago were mostly about her feelings and whenever she exhibited, she felt very exposed. A lot of her creativity now goes into teaching and writing rather than into painting, but that didn't seem such a bad thing. She has had the joy of helping other people to realize some of their own ambitions and aspirations. So the 'block' that stops her painting really is alive, since it is the time she spends on other people's creativity and is a creative activity in its own right. The bit about the hurdle being a good place to grow delicate plants is interesting. When she doesn't paint Sonia tends to write quite a lot. So not painting is 'protecting' her writing, and she actually produces a great deal more when she feels she can't paint.

As for the hurdle, it is used in a garden to protect plants from wind, and it is also something that horses jump over, and that is what it reminded Sonia of when she first drew it. So there is a challenge there that she will have to make some effort to overcome. It is going to take a lot of energy. Well, that's fine. Sonia's current energy is being used to the full, so the painting will have to wait its turn until life is a bit less exciting and demanding and she has lots of energy, emotional as well as physical, to start again. And she feels quite happy to wait, now that she understands this.

The result of this exercise is that Sonia is beginning to appreciate her block and is not so sure that she wants to get rid of it after all! She actually has plenty of paintings already completed for the exhibition, so there isn't, after all, any need to get anxious about it. Instead, she would rather wait until the painting mood comes back upon her naturally, which it usually does after a time. And if it doesn't, does that really matter? No, it doesn't. She feels she has stated all the important things she wanted to state in paint, whereas she still has a lot more to share in words and writing.

This exercise illustrates the point that many of the exercises in this book work in unexpected ways. They don't always solve the problem in the way we might expect them to or even in the way we hoped for. We need to be open to the ideas they generate, whatever those ideas are, and to be flexible in using and understanding them.

ACTION: Don't worry if you're not good at art or at drawing, it's surprising how you can get a general idea from even a scribble. Imagine what a block to your thinking would look like, and then think what colour it might be. Take a coloured crayon or paint in that colour and scribble or scrub paint onto a sheet of paper until it starts to develop some shape. Don't worry if it doesn't look like anything in particular, just keep on filling it in until it looks near to the shape your mental block feels. You might feel that it needs some other colours. If so put them in. You may be able to see immediately what it is. If not, put it away until you can look at it objectively. You could give the picture a title, the more fanciful the better. Look at it and see if it needs anything adding to it. Turn it upside down, sideways. Write down any ideas that come to you. What is your block telling you?

Being the obstacle

If the last exercise hasn't worked for you, another method is to imagine that *you* are the block in your own mind that is stopping you from solving your problem:

> Rob was very interested in fitness and attended his local sports centre regularly. When his closest friend was taken into hospital suffering from cancer Rob organized a sponsored fun-run to raise funds for some equipment that was needed in the cancer ward. He organized a fund-raising committee and persuaded many people from the sports centre to join in the event. But as the time drew nearer he found that he was really regretting his decision. He kept pulling muscles and suffering other slight injuries and eventually told the organizing committee that he was sorry but that he himself wasn't fit enough to take part.
>
> Privately Rob was very puzzled with his own decision. He felt that he should really have taken part in the run but he also felt that something was preventing him, although he wasn't sure what it was. Whenever he tried to think about it he felt sick and tense. Twice he changed his mind and was about to telephone the sports centre to say that he would take part but never quite got round to making the phone call. It worried him so much he started losing sleep and soon found that he was becoming forgetful about all sorts of things to do with his job. He talked it over with a friend who told him that there was no logical reason why he should feel guilty since he had organized the event well and it could go ahead without him.
>
> In a workshop on emotions Rob brought up his problem about the run. He pretended to be the mental block that constantly stopped him thinking clearly or understanding himself:

> > I'm a big dark block in Rob's mind. I am strong and fierce and I am growing all the time. I am alive but I'm not like any

creature that he has ever seen. I stop him thinking clearly by frightening him. I tighten up his muscles and make him clumsy so he will hurt himself and be unable to do the run. I enjoy making him afraid and soon I will grow large enough to stop him doing anything energetic.

The group leader asked Rob why the block needed to do this to Rob. Still acting as the block, Rob answered: 'I must stop him or he will kill himself with all this activity.'

The group leader then asked Rob if this made any sense to him. Rob was quiet for a time and then said that he had never realized that he had a deep-seated fear that he might die of a heart attack. His father had died very suddenly running for a bus when Rob had been quite young. Only after his death was it realized that he had been suffering from a congenital heart condition.

Rob was a policeman so had had a very rigorous physical examination when he went into the police force. He certainly wasn't suffering from the same condition his father had had. But as Rob thought about the problem he realized that, like many people, he also had a deep fear of cancer. His friend in hospital was responding well to treatment but Rob had not been to see him. Suddenly the events connected in Rob's mind: his guilt about not going to see his friend, his own fear of dying of a heart attack. He had never quite come to terms with the fact that one day he himself would die. Having a friend of the same age as himself suffering from what might have been a fatal illness had made death suddenly very real to him. As he continued to think about these connections Rob realized that his father had died at the same age as he now was. The 'block' in his mind, he now realized, was almost like growing cancer cells.

If you have never worked through an emotional block yourself you may imagine that knowing what a block was about would make the situation worse, not better. But insight invariably brings understanding, and so relief:

Once Rob knew what his irriational fears were about, he was filled with relief. He knew his own health was excellent and that there was no rational reason to be afraid of having a heart attack or of getting cancer. He knew, logically, that cancer is not infectious and that there was no risk to himself in visiting his friend. So taking part in the fun-run could only be helpful to everyone: to his friend, to the hospital, to other cancer sufferers and for his own good health and fitness. The block now felt not so much like cancer but more like what it almost certainly was: growing fear of illness. He could understand now how the immature childish emotional part of his mind had tried to protect him from being connected in any way with the cancer hospital and with vigorous exercise. But his adult intelligent mind could now look at these fears and see them as quite inappropriate. He went back into training, visited his friend and participated in the run. Each of these activities made him feel slightly anxious but now that he understood what the anxiety was about he was able to conquer his fears.

ACTION: Find a private place where you can talk aloud without anyone wondering what you are doing. If there isn't anywhere you can do this, try writing it down instead of speaking aloud. Some people find writing easier anyway.

Start off your speaking or writing with 'I am a block in (your own name)'s head that is stopping her/him from thinking clearly and solving this problem'. Then go on and describe yourself. What kind of a block are you? Large or small? Thin or fat? Spiky or rounded? Tough or delicate? Cold or young? Fresh and new or ancient and hoary? What colour are you? Are you alive or inanimate? Are you human, animal, fish or fowl or some imaginary creature from fairy tale or from another planet?

When you have described yourself in detail, imagine that you are now hard at work, doing your job and stopping your self thinking through the problem. How do you do this? Try to imagine that, as the block you are pretending to be, you take pride in your job of stopping clear thinking. So describe how you do this and how well you do this. You may do it by making the person (really yourself, of course) feel too anxious to concentrate, or by making her/him feel guilty, or too tired to be bothered. Say, or write, what you do to the person's body to block them: for example, tightening muscles, making her/him breathe shallowly, giving her/him a headache. And then tell the person why you need to do this. Some mental blocks are very useful; they stop us doing things that could be difficult or hurtful to us, or help us to forget things that seemed very painful at the time. The reason why it's worth discovering exactly what they are about is because blocking out a feeling or a thought may have been quite reasonable at the time but is now no longer valid. So you may be stopping yourself doing something that at one time would have been bad for you but is bad no longer.

Now step back and think about what you have said or written. Try to be open-minded about whatever comes to you. If they are childlike feelings, remember you were a child once but that you are no longer a child and don't need to be afraid; you are an adult now and have control over your own life and can choose how you act.

8

Resolving Conflicts

The Parent-Adult-Child in us. The two chairs/the three chairs. Assertiveness.

The Parent-Adult-Child in us

We were all children once, and many of our childhood experiences and feelings colour our adult life. In part, this is healthy, but sometimes the 'child' in us undermines our adulthood and we don't feel in control of our lives, or adult at all. So even if you are fairly sure of what you want to do, or of what ought to be done, you may feel unable to put it into practice. This can result in some very uncomfortable feelings, where one part of you seems to be saying 'go ahead' and another part is saying, 'No, I can't'. Or you might be dithering between two possible solutions, unable to decide which one is the best. This inner conflict can make us feel tired, anxious, unable to act and even depressed or confused.

The Parent

As young children we learn most things from adults, especially our parents or those people who take on the role of parents in our life: foster parents, house parents, grandparents, whoever brought us up. Some of these messages are obviously spoken, but some are unspoken. For example, we learn that when an adult smiles we are being approved of, whereas when the teacher frowns we know, without being told, that we have got the answer wrong. These messages are added to by other adults who are important to us. They could be teachers, neighbours, shopkeepers, police; people who we see as in authority whether good or bad; adults whom we admire, or fear, or see as wiser than ourselves. All of these ideas are taken into our minds and the bulk of them we assume to be true. Eric Berne, the inventor of Transactional Analysis (see Further Reading), called these Parent messages. He suggests that they stay in our minds like a tape recording or like the script of a play, and a lot of them we remember word for word. Just sit quietly for a moment and

51

remember what one of your parents or parent figures told you. Messages like: 'Don't leave your mouth open or flies will fly in'; 'Don't be stupid!' 'Work hard or you'll never make anything of your life!' 'Don't slouch!' 'Don't eat with your knife.' 'Don't be cheeky!' 'Don't cross the road without looking!' Lots and lots of don'ts, some of them sensible, some of them just upsetting. Some people have a constant stream of these messages, so they are constantly worried by things like: 'Everyone is looking at you!' 'You're no good!' 'You'll never be as bright as your brother/sister!' 'Why can't you be like so-and-so?'

Berne thought that just about everyone has Parent messages in their heads and that a great number of them are 'shoulds' and 'musts' and 'oughts' and 'shouldn'ts' and 'mustn'ts' and 'ought-not-tos'.

The Child

Berne goes on to suggest that there is also a child part of us still existing, even though we know we are really adult. This child part is still trying to be 'good' and trying to please other people or is still rebelling and doing things just to irritate or annoy or to break the rules. He called this the Adapted Child. He says that there is also a Free Child inside most of us; this is the part of our personality that enjoys fun and is lighthearted, or cries at sad films or gets upset if someone is unkind. You may recognize the difference between your adult emotions and your Child emotions by the sort of words you use to yourself. 'It's not fair' is a Child feeling; 'Why me, why can't someone else get blamed?' is another. Child feelings are sulking and pouting, temper tantrums, pretending to be something you're not (even playing at Being Important, which some people manage to do for most of their lives, is a Child way of behaving). You can recognize the Child in other people by sudden mood swings, giggling, refusal to be responsible for themselves. The Free Child is usually very attractive, open, friendly, lighthearted and responsive to your mood but quickly upset if you don't respond to theirs.

Can you think of times when you have felt young, helpless, out of control of things; when you have felt that you have to conform even though you don't really want to? and of the times when you have suddenly done something just for the sheer fun of it? All these could be aspects of the Child within you.

The Adult

Fortunately for the human race we also have an adult part of our personality. This is the part of our thinking and feeling that is sensible, rational, adult and appropriate. Berne says it's like an efficient computer: you feed in information and it comes out with the right answer. That doesn't mean that the Adult is totally non-emotional, but that the emotions we feel as Adult are the appropriate emotions.

ACTION: Write or talk into a cassette recorder or tell a friend what the Parent inside you has to say about your problem (What *ought* or *ought not* to happen, what *must* happen, what people *should* do). Then see what your Child inside has to say (What you *want* to happen, how you would *like* things to be, what *you* need even if it doesn't suit other people). Finally, discover what the Adult in you has to say about the situation (what it would be reasonable to ask for or expect, what your feelings are, how your intelligence tells you that things will probably work out). Then look at or listen to or get your friend to report on all three viewpoints. You'll need to stay in your Adult to do this!

If you're working on this using a cassette recorder, you'll notice that your tone of voice is very different in each of the three aspects. The Parent often has a lofty, superior way of speaking, or a nagging, hectoring voice. The actual words you use may be recognizable and word for word what your Parent-figures said to you ('Now look here.' 'Pay attention!' 'Shut up!' 'Go away!' 'I'm only saying this for your own good!'). The Child often sounds a bit whining or pathetic, the Free Child is often giggly and breathless. Again, the very language you use may be child-like and old stammers or stutters may occur.

Doing this exercise will help to clarify the real issues for you. You can do this exercise at the beginning of problem solving, or you can use it at this stage when you want to check whether the answer you have found is the right one. It also helps you to notice if you are being rather childish and immature, or if you are on your high horse trying to force other people and yourself to do things that just aren't sensible or workable or realistic. The ideal solution is to get the Parent, the Adult and the Child in you to agree on the best solution for all parts of your personality.

Using Transactional Analysis we can separate out very confused feelings:

Ian's problem was that his wife had had an affair with another man. He had always thought of himself as very broad minded and forgiving. But he was shocked to discover that he couldn't forget it and couldn't, in his heart of hearts, forgive her. Miriam had said repeatedly that she was sorry, that it would never happen again, that she had never stopped loving Ian. He came for counselling because he had decided to leave his wife but couldn't quite make the break. Every time he decided to leave he changed his mind: he felt guilty, or he decided that she couldn't manage without him, or he made tremendous resolutions to forget the whole episode and forgive her. Then a day or two later he was tormented with jealousy and anger and decided that he would go mad if he stayed because he couldn't stand the strength of his own feelings.

We can work through each of Ian's viewpoints about his decision to leave:

His Parent said: 'I am disgusted with Miriam. I don't want to be associated with a person like her. What will my friends think of me if I stay with a woman who behaves like that? They will think I'm a wimp who can't keep his wife in order'.

That's very typical of the way we think when we're in our Parent state. Ian's next task was to talk from the Child within him. Not surprisingly, his Child within was very hurt:

'I don't know what I did wrong. Why doesn't she love me any more? I did everything I could to make her happy. [Later Ian reported that even as he said this he was aware that this wasn't altogether true.] She doesn't love me as much as I love her and it isn't fair. I'll go away and she'll be lonely and then she'll be sorry. But where will I go? I'll be even lonelier than her. She might go off with the man she had the affair with and then I'll never see her again and I might as well be dead . . .'

and here Ian began to cry with self-pity. His tears were very different from the adult tears he had shed when he had first told his problem; they were loud and became quite angry, very much as a five-year-old might cry. Ian looked up and smiled, slightly embarrassed by this outburst:

'I had no idea I was so sorry for myself, or so cross.' He remembered an incident when he was a child when his mother had gone into hospital for a time and how angry and upset he had felt, even though he was old enough to understand that she had not been ill to reject him. He thought that some of his feelings were connected with this time.

Then the Adult in him commented on the situation:

'I can understand now that I was afraid that I couldn't cope alone, without my wife. And I didn't like those aggressive feelings I've been having; they remind me a lot of my grandfather who had very fixed ideas about women being faithful and pure, but that men had to be allowed their freedom. He was quite a Victorian in his opinions. He never spoke to one of my aunts because she had lived with a man she wasn't married to. I'd never realized I'd taken on so many of his ideas and now that I realize where those ideas come from I can quite definitely say that I think he was wrong, and that the same standards apply to men as much as to women. So I'm certainly in no position to criticize my wife just because she is a woman. The truth of the situation is that we don't get on well and we agreed a long time ago that we had made a mistake in getting married. To be honest, I would feel too scared to get involved with someone else; one bad marriage is enough for me, I don't want to start the same problems with someone else. If I'd thought I could get away with it, I'd probably do the same thing my wife has done. In some ways I almost admire her. But I know my conscience would trouble me. It's something we just don't agree about; I think marriage should be for life, and that faithfulness is essential. Miriam thinks that I'm old-fashioned. She thinks that I should have an affair as well and that we should go on being married and have relationships with other people.

I think I need to talk to her and explain that I don't feel right about that, it isn't what being married means to me. I suppose I could stay with her and she could go on having her freedom and I could stay faithful, but I don't honestly think I could stand that. The Child in me needs love, and so does the Adult. And however much I tried to control the Critical Parent in me I think it would start criticizing *me* for letting the situation go on. I think that unless Miriam is prepared to change I will probably leave. I feel very sad about that, and I know I'll feel very lonely and regret it sometimes, but unless she wants the same things I do, I don't see how we can go on together'.

Ian's counsellor had to help him to discover what *he* wanted; although her secret hope was that somehow he would find a way to stay with Miriam, since she liked both of them very much. It's very important, if you're helping someone else with their decision making, to remember that you're helping in the *process* of decision making, not making the decision for them. In this case it was apparent that Ian had only been postponing doing what he had felt was the right thing all along; in some senses the decision was already made and his relief at sorting his inner conflict out was very evident.

There's a very quick and simple way to find out if you have already decided, deep down, what you intend to do.

ACTION: Toss a coin! Heads I do this, tails I do that. When you looked at the coin, what did you feel? 'Whew, thank goodness it came down that way!' It seems that this is the choice you really wanted and is perhaps the decision that you were unconsciously trying to decide to follow. 'Bother, I think I'll make it the best of three throws'; it looks as though you really didn't want that solution, so if you're not careful you will find ways of making sure it doesn't happen that way. Look back at Chapter 2 and consider whether you have a 'hidden agenda', or think again about whether your Parent is controlling you or your Child is trying to tell you something.

The two chairs/the three chairs

This is a decision-making method from Gestalt therapy. (See the book list if you want to know more about Gestalt therapy.) I find this works best with three chairs.

ACTION: First decide which is your 'intelligent observer' chair. You might think of this as your 'Adult' chair.

Now rehearse to yourself what decision you are trying to make. This could be from your Child and your Parent points of view. 'I want (Child) to do this, but I ought (Parent) to do that'. Or they could be two equally sensible Adult choices, each with points in favour and reasons for not doing or acting in that way. Allot one of the two remaining chairs to one viewpoint and the other to the opposing idea.

Now go and sit in chair no. 1, and say, aloud, why you think this is the best way to solve your problem. When you have listed all the reasons and feelings and hunches for taking this viewpoint, move into the second chair.

Now say all the reasons why *this* course of action is the best. Allow yourself plenty of time to give your reasons and don't miss out vague feelings, fears or anything that you might feel is a bit irrational; this exercise isn't logic or about being seen as sensible and practical, it's to get hold of all the aspects of the problem.

Go back into chair no. 1 and tell chair no. 2 what is wrong with those ideas. Talk to the chair as though there was a person sitting in it. Tell the imaginary person in chair no. 2 how those ideas are silly, or useless, or won't work; get all your negative thought out in the open. When you've run out of reasons why idea no. 2 is no good, go back into chair no. 2 and tell chair no. 1 why its ideas are no good. Don't hold back your feelings, be as cross or as scornful or as fiendishly destructive as you are able, also be as logical and coldly calculating as you can.

You may find that a sort of dialogue begins to develop between the two chairs which are the warring parts of your own personality. Perls, who used this technique a lot, observed that often there is a part that seems to be controlling and dominating and a part that is whiny and pathetic and seems to give way easily. He called them 'Top dog' and 'Underdog'; you may feel that they are Parent and Child, or they may come out as feelings against thinking or body against mind.

When you feel you have taken the argument between the two chairs as far as it will go, go and sit in the third chair. You are now the Director! From this chair you analyse what the argument was about, as though you are the chairperson at a meeting or the counsellor of two people who are having problems with each other, or a teacher dealing with two difficult children. From this chair you will need to be logical and firm and decisive. If you can see some ways in which both points of view could be amalgamated, say so to each chair and explain, kindly but firmly, what you want each to do. It can be helpful to explain to your two chairs that they are, in fact, one and the same person, so their constant bickering is not achieving anything and is making your life difficult. In your Director's chair you have the right to decide what is best for *you*; having made that decision you can then consider how you can make it comfortable to other people involved, or logically decide that they may have to be a bit uncomfortable with the decision you have made.

Assertiveness and your personal rights

Assertiveness is about standing up for yourself, acknowledging certain rights and accepting responsibility for your opinions. Managing to be assertive is a skill – often a question of knowing what one really wants and striking the balance between aggression and docility. As the following example shows, the chair exercise can help us take control of a situation as we assert our needs and wishes in relation to those of others:

Hugo and Florence were neighbours. The part of town they lived in was rough; there were fights when the pubs closed, break-ins and vandalism were common and elderly people particularly were afraid to go out after dark. The local council decided that something must be done to make the area safer and called a meeting of the people living there to discuss what measures they and the council together could suggest.

The meeting was well attended and it was no surprise to anyone there to discover that one of the worst causes of the problem was racial tension. A series of measures was organized to try to get people to understand and tolerate one another better; one scheme was the setting up of a Neighbourhood Watch scheme with members of both communities. Hugo and Florence volunteered to be on the committee. After the first meeting they walked home together to their flats next door to each other; they had hardly spoken before so were surprised to find that they had quite a lot in common; they both enjoyed growing plants, both liked classical music, both lived alone by choice, both read a lot.

Being on the Neighbourhood Watch meant that they began to see quite a lot of one another and Florence discovered that not all elderly white men were narrow-minded and boring whilst Hugo discovered that young black women could be intelligent and sensitive and quiet and didn't have all-night parties every weekend. They took to calling in to one another's homes occasionally with a plant cutting or a book to lend.

But after a while Florence found that she was becoming irritated with Hugo. They were still on the committee together and the whole neighbourhood scheme was beginning to have unexpectedly good results: people had joined together to turn some waste ground into a community garden, an escort group had been formed to walk home with people from the bus-stop at night, a youth club was being organized. People were painting their houses and flats and planting window boxes and the council had repaired street lights and cleared up rubbish. Florence wanted to stay part of the project, but living next to Hugo it seemed that she would always have to go to meetings and come home from them in his company. People on the committee had started to make a joke of it and asked when they were going to knock their two flats together and get married. She realized that they were only teasing but the remarks made her even more resentful about always being in Hugo's company. It seemed that the only way to get out of the situation was to resign from the Neighbourhood Watch committee so she would see less of him, or hope that something would happen to make him leave. She noticed herself making disparaging remarks about him or belittling his ideas and realized, guiltily, that she was trying to make him fall out with her or resign.

She did the two-chairs exercise to decide whether she should resign from the committee or go on with it and try to suppress her irritation.

In chair no. 1 she said: 'I really ought to go on seeing him. He's old and rather lonely and I know he thinks a lot of me. I can make his life a lot happier if I pop in now and again; after all it's only a few hours a week and it doesn't stop me doing anything else more important. It's probably good for me to think about someone else; I could get very selfish living on my own like this. And if I stopped seeing him he would think all black people are selfish and unkind and that's the whole point of this project, to try to get people to see the good in people of a different race.'

She moved to chair no. 2 and said: 'He's not my responsibility. He must have some relations and if they don't visit him that's probably because he doesn't want them to. Or else they are selfish, so why should I do their duty for them? It's not surprising I don't want to spend my time with an old man anyway, most young people prefer their own age group. OK he was interesting at first, but now he goes on telling me the same old stories about the war and he treats me as though I'm a child. I really resent him telling me I should eat more. It's none of his business if I want to go on a diet. He really doesn't understand women either. It's not his business why I choose to live on my own and have a career. He talks as though there's something wrong with me because I don't want children, and he keeps dropping hints that I should get married and have a family. I don't see why I should have to explain to him that teaching the children I do is quite enough and that if I had children myself I couldn't do it. I'm a really good teacher but

60

when I tell him that he said: "Now, now, don't blow your own trumpet!" That *really* annoys me!'

Back in chair no. 1, Florence thought of some more reasons for continuing the friendship:

'If I fall out with him it could affect the Neighbourhood Watch scheme. We seem to be the two most enthusiastic people on the committee and the others take their lead from us, so what will they think if we fall out? They might just lose heart. So there's more than just me and Hugo to think about here. I hadn't realized how much his remarks about me getting married had got under my skin, though. If I do decide to go on being friendly I'll have to stop him doing that. He doesn't know I'm divorced so I suppose he thinks I've never had a boyfriend. If he'd drop all that I might be able to spend a bit of time with him. Perhaps the trouble is the amount of time I spent with him. That's where I made my mistake, I overdid it and now I'm sorry'.

At this point Florence began to realize that she had been rather more lonely than she had been aware of, and that perhaps she had used Hugo's own loneliness as an excuse to visit him for her own benefit more than for his:

In chair no. 2 again, Florence said: 'I still feel tied down by this routine of always going to the meetings together. It's sometimes a nuisance to have to come home first to collect him when I could go straight from school. It's not as though he's senile or ill or anything. He does his own shopping and goes to his club and he managed without me for years before this scheme began. I'm beginning to realize that I've got in the habit of mothering him a bit. I enjoyed that at first but now it's become too much of a responsibility'.

She changed chairs quickly here:

'That's interesting, I hadn't realized I felt so motherly about him and maybe he dislikes that as much as I dislike him treating me as a child'.

The two points of view were beginning to overlap; that's very often what happens with two-chair work as one side begins to understand the other.

Now Florence went into her 'Director' chair:

'Well, as your social worker I think your two sides of Florence need to talk to one another more. One thing that comes out of all this is that it could just be that Hugo is also feeling a bit tied down with the arrangement, and even if he isn't I think he is intelligent and sensitive enough to understand if you tell him some of these feelings. I don't think it's necessary to break off with him altogether, but I do think it's very important for you and Hugo that you talk about all this and understand one another more. It's really silly for you to come home instead of going straight to meetings; all you need to do is tell Hugo that you'll see him there. It might be a good idea to mention your divorce and that you still feel very vulnerable; I'm sure he would never embarrass you again with hints about finding yourself a nice young man. I think another thing that causes problems between you is your different cultures. He has his pride in Britain and the war here and that doesn't mean so much to you; you find all that British pride terribly pompous and self-satisfied and sometimes it feels as though he is saying that British people are better than any other nation. I think there's a bit of racialism in his: "Aren't you lucky to be in our wonderful country?" and I think there's a bit in you too, Florence. You don't find it very pleasant to be kissed by that pale, creased face and you're not quite sure that his goodnight kiss is as fatherly as he pretends it is. Maybe the people in the Neighbourhood Watch committee are not so far from the truth when they say he's sweet on you. Just because he's nearly old enough to be your grandfather doesn't mean he couldn't fancy you'.

Florence decided that there were more reasons for being a bit cautious about her friendship with Hugo than she had realized. She thought for a day or two about whether her motives were purely selfish and decided that they weren't. She still wanted to be a good neighbour and she still cared for the old man but she realized that if she let things go on as they had done she would be building up a lot of resentment and embarrassment for herself, and in the long run these would be as bad for Hugo as for her. She spoke to Hugo as soon as she felt clearer, and although he was disappointed that they wouldn't be spending as much time together as before, he said he had always realized that it was unlikely that a young woman would want an elderly man for a really close friend.

When she explained about her divorce, Hugo was really upset that he had been so tactless. When committee members started the usual jokes about the two of them he told them that the joke had become very boring and insisted that they promise to stop.

Florence was able to stay on the committee and so was Hugo; their friendship, though cooler, was actually improved when Hugo revealed that he had felt that Florence was giving him advice as though he was a bit senile; he had been quite offended that she thought him unable to get to meetings without her. The two of them proved to be a great strength in keeping the Neighbourhood Watch scheme alive.

9

Checking Out Your Solutions

More than one solution: points for and against. Long-term and short term objectives. Avoiding old unhelpful life patterns.

More than one solution

By now you may well have solved your problem. If you haven't, at least you should have a much clearer notion of all the issues involved and have some creative ideas that you might use in solving it. Indeed, you may have more than one solution which would work, and this poses a new problem: which solution should you use? Here is a method which could help you to decide.

ACTION: List all the points for and all the points against each solution. Make two columns on a sheet of paper with 'pro' (or 'for') at the top of the one and 'con' (or 'against') at the top of the other. Take one of your possible solutions and fill in as many reasons for or against it as you can. When you've completed your list, add at the bottom any other factors that could influence you, even if they're not necessarily in favour or against that idea.

Then do the same for your other or any other solutions. Some will turn out quite naturally to have a great deal more in favour of adopting them than they have points against them and you can see at once that this looks like being the best answer.

Here is an example:

How to spend your day off

You've gone through several possibilities and decided that the only things you really want to do are to visit an exhibition on one of your interests (like the motor show, or a stamp collectors' exhibition or whatever else interests you) or to visit an old friend who lives some distance away. Either would be a pleasant way to spend the day and either would take the whole day, so you can't do both.

Go to the exhibition?

FOR	AGAINST
– learn a lot	– tiring
– might get bargains	– might waste money
– keep me up to date	– might be crowded
– meet other enthusiasts	
– won't be on again for a year	
– always wanted to go	
– could be fun	

NEITHER FOR NOR AGAINST

I'm quite curious about this kind of big exhibition, so it would be interesting to see what it's like even if I don't like it. Once I've been I'd know whether I would want to go again another year and I could stop saying 'One of these days I'll go'.

Visit my friend?

FOR	AGAINST
– good to see him again	– rail fare is dear
– he'd give me lunch	– could go any time
– nice lazy day	– does he want me to visit?
	– am I taking advantage?
	– could be a bit boring
	– he's coming to see me next month

NEITHER FOR NOR AGAINST

Although we always get on well I don't feel desperate to go and see him, it would just provide me with something to do. If I hadn't anything else in mind I'd probably go, but we are intending to spend a weekend together next month.

Looking at these two sets of pros and cons, there are many more reasons for going to the exhibition than not going, and more reasons for *not* visiting the friend than there are reasons for going. Putting in the neither for nor against thoughts at the end seems to help in making the underlying feelings a bit clearer. Unless there is something else that we haven't considered, it looks as though the exhibition is the right choice.

Long- and short-term objectives

In Chapter 4 it was suggested that you made a 'life map' to discover your long-term objectives in life, and to see whether patterns appeared. The kinds of patterns you might discover could be things like regular changes of home or job, lots of impermanent relationships, repeated periods of anxiety, a tendency to get involved with 'lame ducks' or with a particular type of person, etc. Some people are surprised to discover that whenever they succeed at anything they give it up and try something else, or that if they succeed they immediately feel dissatisfied with their achievement and have to attempt something even harder. Others seem to go from one failure to another and observe a tendency in themselves towards taking on things that they know in their heart of hearts won't succeed, or that they are over-stretching themselves. Victim mentality is one such pattern; the person who was treated badly as a child seems to seek out unsatisfactory situations and relationships as an adult, partly because this is the most familiar way of existing.

So, when you are deciding between two seemingly equally satisfactory ways of solving a problem, think about such patterns and make sure that you're not dropping into a too familiar unsatisfactory one again. Unless, of course, your pattern is one of success and satisfaction! In that case, looking for the decision that fitted that pattern would be the best solution! Make sure that your decision, if it's an important one, will help and not take you in an opposite direction.

ACTION: *I suggest that you only consider your problem in this way if this is an important issue for you* and the problem is one that will make a difference to your life. If it's a small matter stick to the decision you've already made and don't agonise about it any longer!

Look back at your life map and your long-term objectives

in life (Chapter 4), and at the list of wants and needs in Chapter 3. Does your solution fit in with your life objectives? Have you fallen into the same old pattern that you noticed in your life plan? Are you going to get short-term satisfaction but be disappointed in the long term?

Taking the example of the day out, if your life pattern was one in which you seemed regularly to lose friends and regret it, you would be wise to consider whether you were giving your friendships enough priority in your life. That might be because you didn't visit them often enough, so you might need to re-think your decision to go to the exhibition. Alternatively, your life pattern might be that you always put everyone else's interests before your own. If you saw that you constantly martyred yourself and rarely, if ever, gave yourself time to pursue your own interests, then maybe going to the exhibition would help you to break out of that pattern and become more self-reliant.

Looking at long-term objectives, if you were coming up to retirement and felt it important to develop some interesting hobbies, then the exhibition would be the best choice. But if your long-term aims in life were to have a better social life and more friends, and to travel more, then the day with the friend would be the best choice, even though there were short-term reasons for going to the exhibition.

10

Making Decisions

**Putting off decisions. 'Awfulizing'. Running your self down.
Kolb's four-minute evaluation circle.**

Many of the exercises already described are about decision
making as well as problem solving – particularly the four
functions of thinking/feeling/sensing/intuition in Chapter 4 and
the two/three chairs exercise and the Parent/Adult/Child
methods in Chapter 8. They not only help you to think about
your problem more clearly, they can usually help you to reach a
decision at the same time. Similarly, the 'pros and cons' exercise
in Chapter 9 is very much a decision-making exercise. Decision
making goes hand-in-hand with problem solving and is often the
last hurdle in finally resolving the problem.

Putting off decisions

Probably the most common reason for putting off making a
decision is a fear of the consequences. A typical situation
involves a potentially difficult confrontation. For example, you
are well aware that you ought to say something to the neighbour
who plays the radio too loud in the garden, but you don't want to
be unpopular, or you are afraid of what they will do or say; your
deputy at work is not pulling his or her weight, but you can't
decide how to approach the matter. If you think about these
situations you will see that it isn't really *making* the decision that
is difficult, it is doing something about the decision once you've
made it. So you un-make it!

This kind of confrontation is even harder if you feel that the
person may suffer from your remarks. How *can* you tell someone
that s/he is going to be made redundant if you know that s/he has
no other income and is unlikely to be able to find another job?
Why should you be the one to tell your close friend that the
reason she is so unpopular is because her personal hygiene leaves
much to be desired? It's easier to tell yourself that you can't make
up your mind what to do than to admit that you do know the

answer to the problem but it's one that you don't want to have to put into action.

Another problem in making the decision about what to do is the fear of having got it wrong. Will you regret it later? Will other people say you should have behaved differently? Even: 'Will I be punished for deciding this way?' Of course, with hindsight, we may have changed many of our decisions if we had known then what we know now. But it's very important to remember that you cannot live your life backwards. You don't know what is going to happen in the future and neither does anyone else. If someone tells you that you should have done something in a different way, your response has to be that you didn't know! You can't go back in time and change it. Some mistakes can be learned from; others no one could have predicted, not with the best will in the world. You are not infallible, you are only human, and sometimes you will make mistakes.

'Awfulizing'

Albert Ellis says that we 'awfulize' our mistakes. We say, 'I shouldn't have done that, or decided that, and because I got it wrong, or the results went wrong, it is awful, terrible, frightful and it should not have happened and it should be as though it didn't happen. We punish ourselves excessively with feelings of guilt and anxiety. These feelings help us to convince ourselves what nice people we are.

If you find that this kind of agonizing about whether you will get it 'right' is your problem, try looking back at decisions you made in the past.

ACTION: Make a list of decisions you made in the past few months. Clothes you chose, clubs you joined, possessions you bought, friends you made, holidays you took, hobbies you enjoy, classes you've attended, parties you did or didn't go to, things you turned down. Now mark each one with a tick for good decision and cross for bad decision and equals (=) for decisions that were neither good nor bad. Make sure that you mark each one by whether it was good for *you*. For instance, if you bought a striped shirt and friends didn't like it that doesn't mean it was a bad decision, it only means that your friends' tastes in clothes aren't the same as yours. Try to be clear about this kind of issue; if deep down you like the striped shirt then that was the right decision and all that is wrong is your lack of courage in sticking to your own choices.

Are there more ticks and equals than there are crosses? If so, it would appear as though you are quite a good decision-maker and should have more confidence in your ability to make satisfactory decisions in the future. If the crosses outnumber the total of equals and ticks, look at each decision that you now regret and consider whether it really matters so much? So you went to Algiers for a holiday and it was too hot and you caught a tummy bug. Is that really so terrible? Did you learn something from the experience? We need bad experiences as well as good ones, otherwise we would not be able to make choices in the future or be able to give other people advice based on our experience. Was there anything good at all about your choice? Was at least a part of the holiday enjoyable? Would your advice to someone else going to Algiers be: 'Don't go at any price' or 'Choose a cooler time of the year and be careful about eating salads'? Could your bad decision help someone else to make a good decision?

Running yourself down

Check very carefully whether you have a tendency to run yourself down. Do you often say things like: 'Trust me to get it wrong!' or 'I don't like any of my clothes' or 'Whatever I do I'm always sorry afterwards'? Are you able to accept compliments? If someone says how well you look or that they like your sense of humour or how good it is to see you, do you deny it and presume that they are just being polite or are after something?

It is also worthwhile to check whether you could possibly have predicted how things would turn out, at the time. When relationships fail, people often say that they should have known what the other person would do, how they would change, about the sides of their personality they had kept hidden, etc. But how, at the time, could you have possibly known these things? If you trusted someone who betrayed your trust, this does not mean that you are a bad person or a poor decision-maker. If the relationship had turned out to be successful you would now be praising yourself for your loyalty. All you can do is to make your decisions in good faith with the facts that are available to you at that time and if things turn out less than perfectly well, that is life, that is being human and fallible. Forgive yourself and get on with the next decision, even if it means taking the occasional risk.

Kolb's four-minute evaluation circle

Since an inability to make a decision stops us taking action, here is a way of deciding what you think and feel and what action you intend taking. It moves us on from decision to action and suggests how you use the action in an experimental way to learn from past successes and mistakes.

It is called an 'evaluation circle'. It's a four-minute way to make a judgment and understand any situation or event that happens, decide what to do about it and act on that decision. If you find it hard to make up your mind (and who doesn't sometimes?) then the evaluation circle is a great way to get yourself to move on to *doing* something instead of agonizing about it.

ACTION: Get a watch or a clock or someone else to time you. *Don't take longer than the four minutes.* Now jot down or get clear in your mind exactly *what* the event is that you are going to think about. In this case it's the possible solutions to the problem. Look at the diagram below to see how it works. You can write down the thoughts you have at each of the stages, or you can just think them to yourself.
1. *Feelings* For one minute only. What do I feel about this? (*in* this case, what do I feel about this possible solution?). Not deep or profound ideas, just the emotions that you have straight away when you think about the solution.
2. *Reflections* For one minute only: reflect on these feelings.
3. *Theories* For one minute only ask yourself: what is my

71

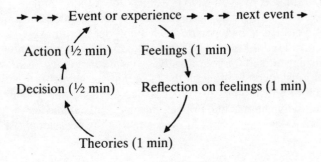

theory or theories about all this? (Theories can be what you thought you thought, what people generally think about this, what you expected to happen, actual theories or research you have come across about this issue.)

4. *Decision*   For half a minute only. What is my decision about this?

5. *Action*   For half a minute only. What action do I now need to take in the light of this decision?

This is an extremely quick and time-effective device for counselling yourself and making decisions. It is useful when you are upset with someone and not able to get your feelings of hurt or anger out of your head; almost invariably it will enable you to move on mentally to whatever you need to do next. Having decided what to do, you can then see the 'trying it out' as another experience which you can evaluate in the same way, rather than a once-and-for-all success or failure. You make your decision, you decide on your action, you try it out as a separate experience and if it goes wrong you don't have to despair, you just evaluate the failure of your action in the same way. Similarly, if it succeeds, you evaluate your success in a similar way, so that you can understand how your theories and feelings have matched up to bring about a good decision and successful action. Life is then a series of experiences and experiments from which you can learn.

Kolb intended his theory as an explanation to improve people's ability to learn and teachers' ability to teach, but the evaluation circle makes his theory useful as a working method and a philosophy of life as well. Like most problem-solving methods, the evaluation circle works better with practice, and you can practice this one on a bus, in the lunch queue, while the baby has a nap, at the end of a meeting, as part of the meeting or whenever a decision needs to be made. You can teach it to colleagues and do it as a group (though the theories part then tends to take a little longer). Perhaps the thing I like most about it is that it promotes a positive attitude, even towards failure!

11

Putting Your Decisions into Action

Celebrating success. Planning your strategy; time management.

Your problem is analysed and sorted into its component parts. Each of the parts may have needed a different problem-solving method and a different kind of solution. Some needed hard work, some practical solutions, some brilliant insight and an unusual approach, some needed advice, some needed the help of others, some needed experts, some turned out not to be your problem at all and some are insoluble and have to be lived with.

If the problem was a very complex one and there turned out not to be a simple and strightforward solution, then having the answers to your problem is not the end of the matter. If, for example, you work in an organization which is having problems, getting the people to solve them together is no simple matter. So even when the solution is found, people may not be prepared to work together to put it into action if they have undergone a long period of unhappiness and dissent. If your problem is a long-term one, like coping with a disabled child, the solution does not lie in a single decision or a single act, it needs long-term planning and a series of strategies, plus a fair amount of flexibility as other events occur which change your original ideas. There may never be a day when you can say 'this problem is over' even though you have solved many of the factors and made things easier or better or more manageable for every one involved. Like a garden, your problem may need continuous care and attention if it is not to revert to its former unmanageable state. Indeed, it may need more than maintenance, it may need good planning and foresight to avoid other problems developing in the future. We'll look at the possibilities of planning to avoid problems in the next chapter.

Celebrating success

Each time you solve a problem, each time you achieve a part of your plan, celebrate it in some way. At the very least make a note of it in your diary with 'Well done me!' Tell your friends, send round an office memo, remind someone else who's involved of how it was then and how it is now. With bigger successes buy a round of cakes or a round of drinks, go out for a meal, have a party. Our education system tended in the past to concentrate on our faults and mistakes and to make us feel embarrassed or unnecessarily modest about our strengths and successes. To this should be added the British habit of understatement through which we grow up to believe that singing our own praises is socially unacceptable and not at all a nice way to behave. We find the confidence of people of other nationalities brash and unpalatable, and they find us hypocritical and are puzzled by our pretence that we can't cope.

These attitudes are mentioned because it's difficult for many British people to have a realistic attitude about their own abilities. They are unable to praise themselves when they've done well and tend to forget their successes and only remember their failures. This is very unhelpful if you're trying to be positive about your life and not discourage yourself every time a problem comes along. It is important to celebrate successes because you then reinforce your own confidence and condition yourself to persist more and to be more ingenious with future problems. Otherwise, you may never realize how much you have achieved and how far you have changed your circumstances. It's a bit like counting your blessings, noticing that things have actually got better. If the problems were very big, progress may have been so slow and gradual that you would never notice the improvement unless you take note of each of the milestones along the way. Keeping a diary may make you very much more aware of the problems that you've solved, or that have sorted themselves out.

Planning your strategy

Strategy planning is just one way of addressing the various things that need to be done to sort out a complex problem. First make yourself a time limit (days, weeks, months or years). Once you have decided on the time limit, then plan what you hope to achieve in half that time. This gives you a useful milestone: you can assess your progress so far, review your plans and see what changes need to be made in them.

Having made some longer-term plans, the next step is to decide how to start. Become aware of how easy it is to put things off until tomorrow, and so start with today. Even if the only thing you do is to make this plan, it's very useful to give yourself a positive feeling that now you have begun.

Now decide what you need to do next. In the coming week, say (but you may need longer than that), fit the plan to your own circumstances. Now put in as many stages as you feel are practical up to the time you will do your half-way-there review.

Then decide on rewards for yourself if each stage is successful, and also what you will do if you don't succeed. Don't give yourself punishments for failing, that isn't the idea at all: give yourself suggestions for alternative ways of proceeding.

Here are two examples, one for an individual problem, one for a group of people:

Problem: What to do about dreary flat.
Solution: Ideal would be to move, but can't afford to at the moment. Second choice: decorate it.
Time period: One year. That's practical; wouldn't get it done in less, but can't bear to think of it being this awful brown any longer than that.
Half-way-there: Six months' time: Will have completed living-room, hope to have done kitchen as well. Bathroom and bedroom not quite so desperate. Review progress so far and make a new estimate of how long it will realistically take to do the other rooms.

Today: Choose a colour scheme.
By the end of next week: Clear out all things never used. Put things rarely used in a box under bed. Buy emulsion paint for walls.
By end of next month: Done paintwork in living room, started on emulsion painting walls. Buy new lampshade and make a wine-bottle lamp. Buy and put up new shelves. Gone round charity shops and found something colourful (shawl?) to put over sofa.

If I fail: In one year: move and endure longer journey to work.

In six months: Do overtime to pay for someone else to decorate. Don't be tempted to start on another room until this one is finished.

Today: Ask Julie's advice on colour schemes.

Next week: Put junk in hall. Ask Fred at work to get emulsion as he lives near the DIY centre.

Next month: Decide to spend whole day decorating. Leave buying lamps etc. until later. Give myself two more weeks to do living room.

If I succeed: In one year: might still move but out of choice not from despair!

In six months: Have a party in my smart new room.

Today: Feel relieved I've made my own mind up.

Next week: Have a friend round Sunday night for Chinese take-away.

Next month: Give myself two weeks off from decorating to enjoy my living-room. Buy a picture for living-room if I can afford it.

Group problems

If a group of people has a joint problem, getting agreement on what should be done is a large task in itself. Here is a strategy for a group to plan and decide together:

Divide into smaller groups of three or four people, each with paper and pens, and answer the following questions:

what is the maximum time we can allow ourselves to solve this problem?

what might we be able to achieve in half this time?

what needs to be started today?

who should do this?

what should be done by the end of this week?

who should do this?

what should be done by the end of this month?

who should do this?

what actions shall we take if any of these fail?

who should take this action?
how can we keep to this plan?
who will be responsible for checking?
what rewards shall we have if we succeed at this stage?

Then get together as a group and compare and discuss your answers until you find a mutually satisfying timetable and set of strategies. If you can't agree, see if there is a possibility of dividing up into separate groups, each of which performs the tasks in their own way. Pin up the agreed timetables, rewards and solutions to failure where they can be seen and check off each stage as you get to it.

For example:

Problem: To get this office tidier and papers filed correctly as a matter of routine and not in bursts of panic when things go missing. (The initial problem was over a missing file and the acrimony amongst staff about whose fault it was. This brought up a deeper problem about responsibility and some bad feeling about people who were lazy or untidy and then blamed someone else when things went missing. So this is a problem-solving session designed to stop further problems from happening).

Agreement: New system to be in operation in one year.

Fail: Need a full-time filing clerk to do it for us.

Succeed: Buffet lunch for us all provided by the firm.

In six months: Should have filed at least half the backlog and have a new system in operation for future files. We should also have a clearer understanding about who does what and maybe some proper job descriptions. Call a review meeting to assess the new system and how it is working.

Fail: Pay someone overtime to get the backlog sorted out. Do we want to keep people who haven't pulled their weight? Get the union to help with job descriptions, take this to management.

Succeed: Go out together for an evening.

Today: Need to decide who is responsible and tell them honestly rather than continue gossiping and making accusations behind their backs. We also need to have a clear agreement from everyone that they are prepared to do their fair share.

Fail: Spend more time on talking this through tomorrow. Ask people who won't co-operate how they suggest the filing is done?

Succeed: Tell each other what a good bunch we are. Support the people who have admitted their inefficiency.

By end of week: Need to have evolved a better system.

Fail: Get an expert on filing systems to advise us. Call in Organization and Methods experts.

Succeed: Everyone gets a new small piece of desk equipment or a pot plant.

By end of month: Need to have the system installed and start on a training programme so that everyone can use and understand it.

Fail: Might have to extend the time if equipment hasn't arrived.

Succeed: Cream cakes with our morning coffee.

ACTION: Write down your problem and your chosen solution(s). Give yourself a time limit for the solutions to be implemented. Write down what you should have achieved by then, what you will do if you fail and what you will do if you succeed. Do the same for a half-way stage: what you will hope to have achieved, what if you fail, what if you succeed, plus what you may need to re-think at this stage. Make a note in your diary that this is a good time to review your progress so far.

Now decide what you can do today, what you can do in, say a week's time, what in a month's time, what in two months and so on. For each plan a strategy for failure and a reward for success.

Pin up your timetable where you will see it and mark off each stage with a big, brightly coloured tick as you achieve it. Write 'JOB DONE' in large, brightly coloured letters when you have worked through the whole process and keep it up until you've completed your next project, to remind yourself that you can solve a problem and follow your solution through to the end!

12

Creative Problem-Finding

Catching problems before they become unmanageable. Looking for interesting problems. Getting an overview.

If you are the kind of person who feels that the only way you can live comfortably is by taking on other people's problems, or if you are the kind of person who likes the challenge of taking on new and hard things to tackle, you won't be short of problems to solve and you are probably quite creative about doing so. You may actually enjoy it. But if you're the kind of person who sees problems as a bad aspect of your life, you may find the idea of problem *finding* quite horrifying.

But this chapter isn't about making your life even harder or about worrying more. It's about catching problems while they are small and of solving them before they become large and unmanageable. It's also about learning to see problems positively, without panic or despair, and most of all, it's about being creative and inventive in your approach to problems as part of a positive way of life.

Catching problems before they become unmanageable

This can be a rather dispiriting activity so you can save it until you are feeling particularly well and positive. Maybe you could do it after you've solved a particularly knotty problem and so are feeling pleased with yourself and successful.

When you move house it's helpful to make a list of everything that needs doing and all the people and services that must be informed: gas board, electric company, post office, your employers etc. All sorts of details about keys and removal times, milk and newspaper deliveries at the new address, who does what, legal matters, insurance; all have to be thought about and dealt with, otherwise some very large problems may arise. Many estate agents give people lists of all these necessary things so that they can avoid getting into difficulties. The list aims to cover all the problems that might occur, so that they can be solved before they happen or dealt with at the correct time. Of course, a list like this can't solve the emotional problems of moving, problems like leaving friends, getting to know new neighbours and the generally unsettled feeling most people have when they move. But even these emotional problems can be dealt with in positive ways with a bit of forethought: inviting old friends to the new home, making an effort to be friendly with neighbours, being aware of the insecure feeling and realizing that it's a perfectly normal way to feel and will wear off in time.

It is a good idea to look at the whole of your present life in a similar way and make an inventory of all the aspects of it that are operating well and could reasonably be expected to continue to operate well in the foreseeable future, and all the aspects that could cause problems.

ACTION: Take four sheets of paper. At the top of the first sheet write 'OK'; at the top of the second write '?'; at the top of the third write 'Definitely need to change' and at the top of the fourth write 'Need to sort out?'

On the OK sheet write a list of all the things in your life that are fine, or reasonably good, or work well for you, and all the aspects of your life that you're happy with and want to keep that way. If you feel that any of them might be likely to change for the worse, underline them and list them on sheet 4 'Need to sort out'.

On the second sheet with the '?' at the top write down anything that you feel is in doubt: things you're not sure of, things that might change for the worse and things that you would perhaps like to change. Again underline any that seem to need some definite action and add them to the fourth 'Need to sort out' sheet.

On sheet 3, the 'Need to change' sheet, list all the things that you know are definitely causing you or are about to cause you problems. Then underline those that you could do something about and add them to sheet 4.

Here is an example of catching problems before they get too large:

Marion was in her fifties. Her two daughters were married with children of their own and her youngest, her son Martin, still lived at home. Martin was anxious to leave and set up home with his girl friend Debbie.

Marion ran a playgroup three mornings a week and worked as a voluntary helper in a charity shop the other two weekday mornings. She spent her afternoons at home doing housework and gardening and occasionally meeting a friend. Her husband, Joe, 12 years older than her, was looking forward to retirement the following year. Although Marion looked forward to their having more time together, she was concerned about the reduction in their income Joe's retirement would bring. They had had a struggle to bring the children up and when Martin left it would be the first time in their marriage that they would have some financial freedom.

These are Marion's lists:

OK:
– the playgroup: enjoy it and feel I've made a success of it
– gardening and, I suppose, housework, especially when Joe is home to help
– marriage to Joe
– Sarah's marriage and children (Sarah is eldest daughter)
– mortgage will be paid up next year.

?:
– will I miss Martin when he leaves?
– Joe's retirement: money shorter. Spending more time together: will he restrict my freedom? – Will I be too old to run playgroup soon?
– Ellen's marriage: they seem so unhappy together? (Ellen is second daughter)
– I'd be happier if Martin married Debbie (his girlfriend)
– ought I to help Martin to find a flat?

Need to change:
– charity shop: don't like the way the volunteers take all the

best goods for themselves, even though they pay for them. Don't really like manageress
- I'd like a paid job, that would solve some financial problems and I'd like to feel I could earn my own living after all these years at home with the family.

Need to sort out:
- how does Joe intend to spend his time when he retires?
- money: I'm not really sure what our income will be
- I'm getting overweight
- we're not getting any younger, we should look after our health better.

There were obviously some very big changes coming in Marion's life. Since she wasn't happy in the charity shop and had been thinking about getting paid work for some time this could be a good time to leave. Instead of worrying about their financial situation without properly understanding it, she had a long talk with Joe about his retirement, their finances and his plans. Without Martin at home they would be reasonably well off, but Joe suggested that maybe her real reason for wanting paid work was more to do with having an interesting career than for money and, to her surprise, he was all for it. He was thinking about running a small business part-time himself when he retired and suggested that they might think about doing this together.

She talked to Martin about her dislike of his living with Debbie without being married, and although Martin said he could understand her point of view, he didn't share it and had no intention of changing his plans. He and Debbie had decided that they would marry if they decided to have a family, and although this wasn't quite as Marion or Joe would have preferred, they agreed that they were perhaps a bit old-fashioned and had different moral views. They both liked Debbie very much and didn't want her to feel that they had anything against her. It turned out that Debbie's parents, too, were anxious about the situation and relieved to hear that Martin's parents felt the same. But Martin and Debbie were adults and had to make their own decisions and Marion realized that this was not, in fact, a matter about which she had much choice. She could either accept the situation or risk losing the friendship of her son and his girlfriend.

Through thinking more carefully about Martin and Debbie she began to realize that there was very little she could do about her younger daughter's unhappy marriage. She wrote saying that she was aware of the situation and that she was available if there was anything she could do to help, but that she realized that mothers are not always the best people to give advice. (Her instinct was to be cross with her daughter and assume she was at fault, largely because Ellen had been rather a handful when she was in her teens!)

She decided to let her children ask for help if they needed her and meanwhile to get on with her own plans. She enrolled at the local technical college for evening classes in modern office skills to update the secretarial training she had had before she married. Joe was interested in the prospectus when she brought it home and decided to enrol on a computer course as this might be useful if his small business ideas came to fruition.

She saw her doctor about her weight problem and he suggested that she and Joe had check-ups before they started on any fitness programme. This turned out to be really important for Joe as he was found to have a mild heart condition which neither of them had suspected. Regular light exercise was now really important to maintain his health in his retirement.

By the time Joe retired, Marion had completed her course and discovered a real aptitude for word processing. She sold her share in the Play School and put the money towards buying equipment for a small secretarial agency she could run from home, using Martin's now empty bedroom. Her weight wasn't very much reduced but she was much fitter because of the daily walks and the once-a-week swim she and Joe took.

Ellen's marriage did break up. This was a sad time for all the family but Marion was relieved that she had the interest of her business to keep her from worrying unnecessarily and un-productively.

Joe never did start his own business, though he helped Marion with the accounts for hers. He became fascinated by computer games and wrote programmes for several, and started a computer club. However, he took over most of the housework, much to Marion's surprise, and taught himself to be a very good cook. The new arrangement, with Marion as wage-earner and Joe as housekeeper, suited both of them extremely well, even though some of their friends teased them about the role reversal.

Joe died three years after he retired. Marion felt that he had been able to enjoy his few years of retirement and express a side of his personality that neither of them had realized was there. Her business now became the centre of her life. It didn't altogether solve her loneliness nor stop her missing Joe, but at least she was more self-sufficient, financially and emotionally, than she had been when she started to look at some of the problems that might be looming in her life.

Looking for interesting problems

Ruth and Dorothy spent an hour trying out ways of hanging drip-dry shirts on the clothes line so that they wouldn't need much, if any, ironing. It wasn't a very serious session as they both had young children so were constantly interrupted. But that hour saved Ruth countless hours of ironing in the following years. It also made hanging washing out more interesting as she tried out different ways of hanging other clothes and continued to experiment with the shirts. That's an example of actively looking for a problem and solving it creatively.

(In case you're interested, the method they chose was to fasten the top button and peg the bottom open at each side seam and both fronts with four pegs. This keeps the front stretched out smoothly, the collar keeps its shape and the wind can blow down the sleeves and de-crease them. Dorothy thought the whole exercise a waste of time; she didn't really want to think about such a dull job, so she went on ironing shirts for years.)

I was in a local adult education centre when I overheard two Open University students. One was telling the other that she knew she had read a book which would be useful to quote in her essay, but that she couldn't remember the author or title, or where she'd borrowed it from. I was about to start on a course of study myself and realized I might have a similar problem, especially as I have a rather poor memory. I had already been given a rather nice 'mini-index' file: a small loose-leaf book with alphabetical divisions. So from the very start of my course I made a note of every book I heard of or read connected with my course. I made the main entry under the author's name and invented a simple code so I'd know where the book came from: L for local library, U for the university library, D for the friend who lent me a lot of books etc. (I made a list of my code letters at the back, since I know I'm quite capable of forgetting what my own code means!) Then I made entries for the main topics or subjects covered in the book. Most only needed one. So a typical entry would be, in the 'P' section: *The Philosophy of Education* see Schofield. In the 'S' section I had the full entry: Schofield, H. *The Philosophy of Education*. Allen & Unwin, 1972. B. The 'B' meant that I owned a copy myself. This was a quick and simple system that saved me hours of library searches and made the booklist that had to accompany every essay a much easier matter. The smallness of the file meant that it could stay in my pocket or handbag so I could quote from it during discussions and carry it into the library with me when I was studying. My only anxiety was that it would discourage me from memorizing things and so make my memory even worse. The surprise was that it had the opposite effect and I can still remember the names and authors of all the major books I read on the course and even where I borrowed them from.

What systems could you start for yourself that would make your working or home life easier or more interesting? Don't discount the importance of making things interesting, even if they take more time. Boredom makes people unhappy, dull, stressed and unhealthy, so there are times when making a job more complicated can be beneficial. What do you do that you have always done that way without considering why? What do you do the way one of your parents taught you to do it? What systems do you have at work that are done that way because that is the way they have always done them? Could there be a better way, or a way that suits you better?

Look at your environment. Would your place of work be cheerier if there were some colourful posters on the walls? Does it have to be dirty, or untidy; would a good clean-up make it pleasanter for workers and customers? Would you feel more satisfaction and pleasure in your work if it was done better or presented in a new way? Do tools and equipment go missing in your home or at work? Would some time sorting them out and organizing a new system of storing them make life easier in the long run, even if it meant spending extra time now thinking about it and setting the system up? Would you feel more inclined to do repair jobs if your tools or sewing materials were neatly in order rather than jumbled up together, if tools were clean and sharpened, sewing cottons wound on their bobbins rather than in the more usual tangled up knot?

Pay attention to those tasks that are regularly irritating, or boring, or difficult for you, or confusing, and address your mind to the possibility that they could be seen as a curable or at least an improvable problem. Trying not to be annoyed with a bad system takes up a lot of emotional energy that would be better used in trying to invent a new method.

ACTION: Write down the answers to the following questions:

What irritates me regularly?

What do I feel I do badly: is it really me or is it the way I do it?

What could I do better if I had a better way of doing it?

What could I do more elegantly? (by elegantly, I mean to suggest the idea of flowing smoothly from one activity to another with skill and finesse!)

When you've answered these questions, ask yourself the following questions about each of the issues you have identified as needing some creative problem solving:

How would I do this if I had never seen it done before, if I was doing it for the first time in the history of the world?

How would I do this if I was completely alone with no one else to please and no one else to criticize my way of doing it?

How would I do this if I wanted to do it *less* well? How could I make this task even more boring/difficult/confusing for myself? (This may give you some clues as to what is hard about it and identify the aspects that are the ones that cause you problems)

What do I need to learn, to do this task better? Which parts of this activity are the parts that need changing? Which bits work right and can stay the same?

What other activity or action is similar to this one? Can I take some aspect of the other activity and use it to improve this one?

Creativity is not a special gift that only artists and inventors have. Almost everyone is creative in some way and finding original solutions to even small problems can make life more satisfying and interesting. I think it is very creative to find a new way of doing something even if you discover that someone else has had the same idea; it was original for you and you should give yourself credit for working it out for yourself.

Actively looking for creative problems and solving them creates stimulation and challenge and gives you an opportunity to be much more in control of the quality of your life. It's a very positive way to live.

Getting an overview

It's not easy to see where problems in your life could surface, or which areas of your life need some positive re-thinking, whilst you are in the middle of it all. A friend who has been very ill recently told me that he was almost glad of the illness because the period of non-activity had made him think about the whole of his life rather than the immediate everyday problems that take up most of our waking hours. So although things like the Life Plan in Chapter 4 are intended to help you to take a longer view, or unless you are one of those unusual people who can be objective and seemingly distance themselves from feeling submerged in what is happening now, how is it possible to get an overview of your life without having to make yourself seriously ill?

Some people find that holidays are the time when they can take a look at their lives and what they're doing. It may take about four or five days to relax before that moment comes when one can say to oneself: 'What is it all about? What am I all about? Is this how I want to be spending my time?'

But not everyone can afford holidays, or is able to get away from their home situations. Even so, a day away can be enough. Going to a completely different environment can, if you choose to use it in this way, be a chance to think quietly about your life. You may need to plan in your mind that you will do this, so that you make time to be quiet with yourself or with a trusted companion.

Counselling or psychotherapy can also provide you with a time 'outside' your normal life in which you take stock. You could ask a counsellor or therapist if they would be prepared for you to use your time with them in this way, rather than in the more usual examination of your past life and its effects on your present.

Many people find that meditation performs the same function: in the deep peace and quiet of the meditative state can be found the feelings of distance and objectivity necessary for a re-think.

There are many other ways in which people can take an overview of their lives. The experience of something profoundly moving or artistic or religious can have this affect. Music, paintings, sculpture, a piece of theatre, a television play, something very beautiful, a profound piece of writing, all these and others have probably, at times, had the effect of taking us into another kind of experience. And from that experience our own life has seemed different. Herbert Marcuse, the philosopher, said that art tears the veils between us and another reality; the reality of passion and intense feeling which we cover up with the social fabric of everyday intercourse. That may seem a long way from hanging up shirts or running a secretarial agency. But the arts immerse us in the creative reality that we can do things differently, imaginatively, even excitingly. We can change, and we can change what we do and we can change the ways we do things.

13

Problem Solving With a Group

You may wish to use some of the exercises in this book with a group of people. There are a lot of advantages in doing this. You can help one another to understand the method; you get a greater variety of viewpoints; a group of people can come up with a lot more ideas if you are trying to think of creative solutions to problems. You can learn a lot more about each other and understand one another better if you realize the problems others have; this is particularly useful if you actually work together or meet together regularly. You feel better when you realize that other people have problems, even if they are very different from your own.

Many of the difficulties of working with a group, can be ironed out if you start off with some clear ideas about how groups operate. This is an example of sorting out possible problems *before* you begin! There is a list of 'Ground Rules' as Appendix 1 and 'Levels of Confidentiality' as Appendix 2. The Ground Rules aren't really rules, they're more like guidelines. The idea of the ground rules is *not* that the person running the group sets them as rules, but that the group discuss them and decide which are useful and which are not, and add any that they feel are necessary. So they become the group's rules, not the group leader's. You'll find that some of these are totally inappropriate for your group, but they are included so you can pick and choose. Confidentiality is very important when you are sharing personal problems. Even though not everyone is capable of keeping total confidentiality, it's really important to discuss this. You may have to decide to restrict your group's problem solving to imaginary problems or to problems that people don't mind being discussed with others. Then if someone discloses something personal they will realize the implications, and maybe ask others to respect that particular confidence. It does give people the chance to decide just what they are prepared to share. Sometimes groups are very reluctant to discuss confidentiality because they realize the amount of gossip that has been going on in and around the group; in this case it's really important that the group leader insists on some agreement being made and makes sure that everyone is clear about what has been agreed.

If you haven't much experience of teaching or running groups with adults, don't make the mistake of thinking that you can keep a problem-solving session impersonal and unemotional. Most of the methods in this book involve getting in touch with emotions, and even those that don't, may spark off deeper feelings. If you had difficulty with any subject at school, just spend a moment thinking about how strongly you felt and still feel about the times you got poor marks or failed exams or were treated unfairly. A problem-solving group also needs to be very sensitive to the feelings of people who feel that they just aren't any good at solving problems. The people who have a gift for seeing possible answers quickly can add to their feelings of inadequacy, just by being so helpful! So share the idea of looking after one another with the whole of your group.

You may well have a group already formed that wants to do some problem-solving sessions; if you know one another well then you may not need to limit the number of people in the group. But if you don't know each other, six or seven people would be large enough for everyone to have time for their problem. You'll need to spend at least an hour in the first session getting to know one another. Ask each person to tell the group his/her name and a bit about him-/herself, what sort of problems s/he'd like to work on, what s/he is hoping to get out of the group sessions and what s/he feels s/he can offer to other people in the group (like being a good listener, practical help or advice, ideas, making coffee, being the organizer, having a meeting at your home etc). Arrange a set number of sessions; probably six two-hour sessions would be enough to do some of the exercises. Spend the last hour reviewing whether the group feels it has been a success and give each person a chance to say what s/he has learned from it. You could make a list of things that worked well and difficulties that arose so that if another group started, it could benefit from your experience.

Appendix 1

Ground rules

Example

These ground rules or guidelines are for use in *this group only*. They are for discussion and negotiation so that group members know what has been decided and agreed. It should then be possible for the group to become self-regulating and not dependent on the leader/tutor/facilitator to set standards. Outside this group it isn't the social norm to comment on other people's behaviour as this can lead to hurt, misunderstanding and anger, and to you being seen as an aggressive or interfering person. If you wish to set up similar ground rules for any situation, you need to negotiate them with all people concerned and be aware that the terms will end when the situation ends; different 'rules' apply when you meet outside.

No violence   Including verbal violence as defined by the group.

No put-downs   This includes putting your self down. You may decide to draw other people's attention to this.

Honesty   Try to be honest with yourself and in reporting back ('feedback') to others on how they appeared to you. It's not possible to learn from false praise.

Respect for others   This includes keeping *confidentiality*, however we define it. Feedback can be given honestly with kindness and awareness: 'It may be difficult for you to hear this . . .' It includes being able to disagree, and also recognizing that the other person has the right to feel differently. It includes *checking out* rather than making assumptions: 'When you said . . . did you really mean. . . ?' 'Am I right in thinking that you feel. . . ?' *If in doubt, check it out.*

Interrupting and dominating   What guidelines do we want to set about these?

Gossiping   We won't discuss anyone who isn't here and we won't talk about people who are here as if they weren't ('Does he take sugar?') We make statements to the person as far as is reasonable.

Generalizations   Be aware of blanket judgments: 'Everybody feels . . .' may not be true. Equally, be aware if others include you in their generalizations: 'Everyone else in this group may feel like that but I don't'.

'I' language   A lot of people express themselves in the third person: 'You feel silly if . . . don't you?' This can be a family habit and is a way of trying to feel that what I do is the same as what everyone else does. Some people use 'one' in the same way. Learning to talk in 'I' language helps you and other people to understand what is special and unique about you. 'I feel . . .' is also useful, especially if you're not accustomed to express your feelings or to differentiate between thinking and feeling. A group can change radically when the people in it start using the language of 'I' and of feeling; the interaction between people is enriched and far more information is available.

Autonomy   No one has to say or do anything they don't want to. Everyone is responsible for him-/herself and his/her own behaviour. Everyone has the right not to take part in any exercise, or to leave, or to question, or to express feelings, or to ask for more information, or to say I don't understand. We agree not to pressure anyone, even if we feel it is for his/her own good. If individuals *want* to be pressured by the group or the leader, they have the right to ask for this and equally the group and leader have the right to refuse.

Time   We will start and finish on time unless we negotiate changed timing. We won't expect explanations if you're late; we all have lives outside this group which may be more important on occasion. If you decide to leave the group it will be very helpful if you tell us that you are leaving or have left.

Appendix 2

Confidentiality

Example

Below are levels of confidentiality. They set out what can and cannot be discussed with people who are *not* in this group, and what can be discussed with the people in this group when the group isn't meeting. Please discuss each level and whether you think it is right for *this* group. All groups are different, so we aren't looking for rules for all groups, just what you will be happy with if we all agree to it. If other people want a less confidential group than you do, you will need to be more careful about what you disclose in this group.

It is essential to be sure that everyone in the group has indicated their agreement to whichever level we decide on as a group.

1. *Total confidentiality*
Nothing that happens in this group is to be discussed with anyone at all who is not a member of this group.
Possible additions:
a) Nothing that happens in the group should be discussed *even with another group member*, except during group meetings.
b) No one may reveal who is and who isn't a member of this group.
c) You may discuss the group with specific people, as decided by the group, e.g. your counsellor or therapist, your partner, a named colleague, a close friend etc.

2. *Own disclosures only*
You may discuss anything you yourself have said or done in the group, but you may not discuss anything anyone else says or does.
Possible addition:
a) You may only discuss your own contributions with specific

people, as decided by the group, e.g. your counsellor or therapist, your partner, a named colleague, a close friend etc.

3. *Disclosing process and learnings*

You may only discuss exercises, learning materials, methods of facilitation, interpersonal processes, group dynamics and other theoretical matters.

4. *Not disclosing identities*

You may discuss anything that happens in the group but you must not identify anyone by name, occupation, sex, or any other identifying feature.

Possible addition:

a) If someone feels that something s/he says or does is particularly confidential, s/he will tell the group before the end of the session and members will then undertake not to reveal it outside the group.

5. *Open*

You may discuss anything that happens in the group with anyone. You can add:

a) Special issues.

6. *Secret or confidential information*

Specific information, as decided by the group, must not be revealed to people outside the group, except those people the group decide on.

The group leader's confidentiality

Group leaders/tutors/facilitators often have a duty to report on the progress of a group or to report on individual members. They also have supervisors with whom they discuss their work, or are members of peer groups with other group facilitators, where they discuss their work. Group members need to make sure that they are clear about the group leader's confidentiality and how far it extends.

Reality

Some people, with the best will in the world, are unable to keep total confidentiality, however hard they try. Trust may be more appropriately given to their reporting events in a sympathetic manner than to their reliability about not disclosing to others.

Some people need to talk things over with another person before they can understand or assimilate ideas. One answer is to set up networks of group members to meet outside group time. Another answer is to accept people's need to talk things over outside the group and make it part of the negotiation of confidentiality levels.

Effect of confidentiality levels on the group

The higher the degree of confidentiality, the more intense the emotional level of the group can go. If a group don't want confidentiality at all, or only a very slight degree of confidentiality, it is unusual for the group to go into emotional issues in any depth; such a level would be right for a task or learning group working at a mainly intellectual and practical level. A therapy group would need a much higher level for people to feel safe, probably 1 or 2.

Further Reading

Assertiveness

Dickson, A. *A Woman in Your Own Right.* Quartet, 1982.
Paul, N. *The Right to be You.* Chartwell-Bratt, 1985.

Dream Work

Faraday, A. *Dream Power.* Hodder & Stoughton, 1972.
Gendlin, E. *Let Your Body Interpret Your Dreams.* Chiron, 1986.

Four Functions

Jung, C.G. *Man and His Symbols.* Aldus, 1964.

Gestalt Therapy

Pearls, F. *Gestalt Therapy Verbatim.* Real People Press, 1969; Bantam, 1971
Pearls, F., Heffetlind, R. and Goodman, P. *Gestalt Therapy.* Souvenir Press, 1951.
Schiffman, M. *Gestalt Self-therapy.* Self-therapy Press, 1971.

Groups

Houston, G. *The Red Book of Groups.* Rochester Foundation, 1984.

Mind Maps and Thinking Skills

de Bono, E. *Letters to Thinkers.* Penguin, 1968.
Buzan, T. *Use Both Sides of Your Brain.* Dutton, 1983.

Rational-emotive Therapy

Ellis, A. *A New Guide to Rational Living.* Englewood Cliffs, 1975.

Transactional Analysis

Berne, E. *Games People Play.* Penguin, 1967.
          What Do You Say After You Say 'Hello'? Corgi, 1975

Stewart, I. & Joines, V. *TA Today: A New Introduction to Transactional Analysis.* Lifespace, 1987.

Index